From Theology of Transparency to Theology of Coexistence

ACADEMIC

I have had the privilege of knowing Dr. Zaki since he was a seminary student and can testify to the incredible way in which God has used him to positively impact the church in Egypt and Egyptian society as a whole. This carefully written book reveals the theological, social and political principles which he espouses and how they can help us understand and impact the Egyptian and Middle East scene with a biblically based approach. Dr. Zaki's holistic approach, based on his understanding of the kingdom of God, is essential in a context where Islam has been promoted as the answer to *all* our needs, whereas the gospel as only meeting our spiritual and eternal needs.

Ramez Atallah
General Director,
The Bible Society of Egypt

This book is a must-read for anyone who wishes to understand events in Egypt, especially in the last fifty years, and the implications for Christian witness and ministry in the largest Arabic-speaking country in the world, as well as in the Middle East more broadly. The author, Andrea Zaki, is one of the most authoritative and influential evangelical statesman of his generation in the Middle East.

In a text characterized by penetrating and sharp analysis, deep historical awareness, and balanced reasoning, Dr. Zaki argues that transparent dialogue and compassionate societal engagement are essential characteristics of Christian witness, especially in Islamic cultures. We would do well to heed his prophetic call to exit our Christian ghettos and engage in transparent verbal witness and dialogue, together with compassionate involvement with others, especially with the downtrodden, marginalized poor and vulnerable, irrespective of their cultural and religious background.

Lindsay Brown, DD
International Director, Lausanne Movement
Former International General Secretary,
International Fellowship of Evangelical Students (IFES)

This book is a sophisticated wrestling with the nature of Christian mission by the head of the Protestant Churches in Egypt and also the head of the largest non-governmental social service agency in Egypt. Zaki integrates an extensive analysis of the ever-developing field of community development with a careful understanding of holistic mission from a solidly biblical perspective. The amazing success of Zaki and his organization in improving Muslim-Christian relationships in Egypt points the way for how to do the same, not only across the Arab world, but everywhere around the globe. An important book.

Ronald J. Sider, PhD
Distinguished Professor Emeritus,
Theology, Holistic Ministry and Public Policy,
Palmer Seminary at Eastern University, Lansdale, Pennsylvania, USA

This book is one of the most exciting and enlightening monographs that has appeared during the last decade. In this relatively concise book, Dr. Zaki engages contemporary theological, political, and sociological scholarship with practical experiences from the church in Egypt, a country of a majority Sunni Muslims. Frequently, Zaki draws practical lessons from his work experience in CEOSS, and from the unique experience of the Egyptian church during the Arab Spring.

Dr. Zaki offers several possible models that could represent the relationship of the church and its responsibility towards society. He is enthusiastic about the holistic model, which includes on the one hand preaching the gospel and on the other hand manifesting the message of the gospel in practical ways – by serving the poor, the marginalized and bringing justice to the oppressed. Zaki warns the church about the lack of transparency of an approach which adopts a hidden agenda, usually by using social services as a net to fish for new congregants. On the basis of the theology of creation, redemption and the kingdom of God, Zaki urges the church to adopt the coexistence model of living through which we seek to live with the "other" as salt and light, to serve and exercise the message and mission of God towards the world and people.

In my view, the model of transparent coexistence offered by Zaki's book breaks the ongoing theological and socio-political debates which keep asking the traditional questions – "evangelism or social action," "secularism or theocracy?"

Congratulations for such a great contribution.

Atef Gendy, PhD
President,
Evangelical Theological Seminary in Cairo, Egypt

From Theology of Transparency to Theology of Coexistence

The Challenge for the Egyptian Christian

Andrea Zaki Stephanous

© 2021 Andrea Zaki Stephanous

Published 2021 by Langham Academic
An imprint of Langham Publishing
www.langhampublishing.org

Langham Publishing and its imprints are a ministry of Langham Partnership

Langham Partnership
PO Box 296, Carlisle, Cumbria, CA3 9WZ, UK
www.langham.org

ISBNs:
978-1-83973-222-5 Print
978-1-83973-464-9 ePub
978-1-83973-466-3 PDF

Andrea Zaki Stephanous has asserted his right under the Copyright, Designs and Patents Act, 1988 to be identified as the Author of this work.

All rights reserved. No part of this publication may be reproduced, stored in a retrieval system or transmitted, in any form or by any means, electronic, mechanical, photocopying, recording or otherwise, without the prior written permission of the publisher or the Copyright Licensing Agency.

Requests to reuse content from Langham Publishing are processed through PLSclear. Please visit www.plsclear.com to complete your request.

Scriptures taken from the Holy Bible, New International Version®, NIV®. Copyright © 1973, 1978, 1984, 2011 by Biblica, Inc.™ Used by permission of Zondervan.

British Library Cataloguing-in-Publication Data
A catalogue record for this book is available from the British Library.

ISBN: 978-1-83973-222-5

Cover & Book Design: projectluz.com

Langham Partnership actively supports theological dialogue and an author's right to publish but does not necessarily endorse the views and opinions set forth here or in works referenced within this publication, nor can we guarantee technical and grammatical correctness. Langham Partnership does not accept any responsibility or liability to persons or property as a consequence of the reading, use or interpretation of its published content.

Contents

Foreword ix
Preface xi
A Note on the Arabic Transliteration xiii

1 Egyptian Society and the Church 1
   The Church in Egypt 3
   Political Islam 8
   The Challenge of the State of Israel 15
   The Clash of Civilization 19
   The Arab Spring 29

2 The Church and the Kingdom of God 37
   The Kingdom of God in Modern Interpretations 38
   Salvation or Social Action? 48
   The Theology of Samuel Habib 55
   Models for Christian Engagement 60

3 The Church and Coexistence 67
   Church, Citizenship, and Coexistence 68
   The Theological Basis for Coexistence 70
   Religion and Power 75
   Religious Pluralism, Dialogue, and Mission 77
   Religious Freedom and Coexistence 80

4 Evolution of Developmental Action 83
   The Evolution of Conceptual Understanding of Development
      Action in Egypt 84
   The Concepts of Growth and Development 90
   Evolution of Inclusive and Sustainable Development Strategies ... 93
   Facing the Future 101

5 Locally Based Initiatives 103
   A Brief History of CEOSS 104
   CEOSS Example Initiatives 114
   The Impact of CEOSS 163

6 Conclusion 165

   Bibliography 171

Foreword

In 2011 and 2012, waves of social upheaval and revolution brought Egypt to the brink of the abyss. The most remarkable evidence of the resilience of the Egyptian people is that they went right up to that brink . . . then – amazingly – they pulled back.

Egypt survived a year of oppressive Muslim Brotherhood government and months of violent protests, culminating on 30 June 2013 which is now called the people's revolution. The nation adopted a democratic constitution, and Egypt is now a strong, stable, and prosperous nation.

Dr. Andrea Zaki had a front-and-center seat throughout those traumatic events. He has a deep understanding of Egypt's history and culture as well as Egypt's social and spiritual problems. From a very young age, Dr. Zaki has demonstrated leadership skills and gifts that have been recognized by leaders both inside and outside of Egypt.

In 1997, a dear friend of mine, Dr. Samuel Habib, went to be with the Lord. He was the founder of the Coptic Evangelical Organization for Social Services (CEOSS). Later, Dr. Andrea Zaki was chosen to lead that organization. God has used Dr. Zaki in a mighty way to guide CEOSS into the twenty-first century.

CEOSS was founded out of a desire to spread the good news across Egypt – good news for the poor, freedom for prisoners and the oppressed, and healing for the suffering and blind (see Luke 4:18). In his tenure as president of CEOSS, Dr. Zaki has ably and effectively widened the ministry and deepened the impact of that organization throughout Egypt.

My old friend, the late John Stott, told me that when a ministry tries to combine evangelism and the "social gospel," the social gospel eventually becomes dominant and evangelism fades from the scene. He cited a number of examples through history. But under Dr. Andrea Zaki's leadership, his ministry has proven to be the exception to John Stott's rule.

As you will discover in this book, Dr. Zaki has successfully maintained a rigorous balance between the spiritual and social dimensions of the gospel. He rightly understands what so many leaders have forgotten: Jesus preached one gospel, not two. His gospel was the good news of salvation and eternal life – *and* the good news of compassion for the needy and oppressed. These two dimensions of the gospel are no more in conflict than the two sides of one coin.

That is why this book is a must-read! It is important not only for those who are interested in the Middle East and Egypt, but for all who seek to live as witnesses for Christ in a non-Christian culture, surrounded by non-Christian neighbors. In these pages, you will learn how to live peaceably and how to minister successfully, even against the odds and when the contexts are different.

I have observed first-hand how Dr. Zaki relates to leaders of Muslim institutions at the highest level. I have seen how lovingly and graciously he communicates with such leaders as the Grand Mufti of Egypt and Egypt's Minister of Islamic Affairs, and even His Excellency President Abdel Fatah El Sisi. I have seen how Muslim leaders have responded to this boldly evangelical Christian leader with genuine admiration and respect.

In a time when strong leadership role models are in short supply, this book gives us a contemporary role model of balanced Christian leadership. I recommend – no, let me put it more strongly! – I *urge* you to read Dr. Andrea Zaki's important book, *From Theology of Transparency to Theology of Coexistence*. May God use its message to touch your heart and change many lives.

Rev. Michael Youssef, PhD

Preface

In the last few decades, the relationship between religion, politics, and social services have become complex and tangled. We have found that many of those who work in social services have ulterior motives, some of them using the needs of the people to serve their own purposes. I have attempted to analyze a number of subjects within this text.

The first chapter provides a critical reading of the progression of Egyptian Christian thought as it relates to the church's relationship with Egyptian society, as well as the evolution of that relationship in response to current events. Though this relationship is historic (more than two thousand years old) and worth overview, the focus of this section will pertain specifically to changes in the last fifty years – and the implications of events occurring in the first two decades of the third millennium.

In the second chapter, I attempt to arrive at a holistic understanding of the kingdom of God and how such an ethic might shape the mission of the church in Egypt. Is salvation for this life only or for the next life as well? Is it meant for the human body in the "here and now" or eternally in the kingdom to come?

The third chapter discusses the concept of "coexistence" – that is, the process by which a person or group learns to live alongside people practicing a different way of life than their own. The goals of coexistence include acceptance of diversity, an ability to engage effectively with diverse individuals, and the maintenance of a positive relationship with this "other" person or group of people.

In the fourth chapter, I discuss the numerous potential benefits of the social resilience approach to local development and the validity of such efforts in contemporary Egypt.

Finally in chapter 5, I introduce the Coptic Evangelical Organization for Social Services (CEOSS) as the model of a non-profit organization seeking to improve the quality of life for disenfranchised and impoverished local populations through community development, the promotion of justice, equality, and citizenship, and the provision of accessible services to all Egyptian citizens with no discrimination whatsoever on the grounds of gender, faith, or creed.

I am grateful to the many people who have helped me in this research, and I would like to specifically thank Margarite Sarufim and Gihan Eid who helped in collecting materials for development. I would also like to thank Samira Luka and Heba Yousry for their efforts in collecting materials related to intercultural dialogue.

Also, I'd like to give thanks to the team who worked on the text: Fady Atef Mekhael for his efforts as my research assistant; David Victor, who worked on editing the final copy including citations; and Sean Amato for helping in language review and proofreading. I want to thank Lucia Rabbat, the head of my office, for all her time spent coordinating efforts between the members of our team. Finally, I am grateful to Langham Partnership for supporting my theological endeavors and publishing this work.

Andrea Zaki Stephanous
Cairo, Egypt
December 2020

A Note on the Arabic Transliteration

I used many Arabic names and references in this book, and as such I have romanized the Arabic letters. Please see the system of Arabic transliteration (below) that is used in this text.

Arabic Transliteration Alphabet

A a - a Ā ā - ʼ	أ ‎_‎ آ ‎ا‎ ‎_‎ ء	Ḍ ḍ	ض
B b	ب	Ṭ ṭ	ط
T t	ت	Ẓ ẓ	ظ
Th th	ث	ʻ	ع
J j	ج	Gh gh	غ
Ḥ ḥ	ح	F f	ف
Kh kh	خ	Q q	ق
D d	د	K k	ك
Dh dh	ذ	L l	ل
R r	ر	M m	م
Z z	ز	N n	ن
S s	س	H h	ه
Sh sh	ش	W w - u Ū ū	و ‎_ُ‎ و
Ṣ ṣ	ص	Y y - i Ī ī	ي ‎_ِ‎ ي

1

Egyptian Society and the Church

A Critical Reading of the Christian Presence in Egypt

This chapter provides a critical reading of the progression of Egyptian Christian thought in regards to the church's relationship to society. Though this relationship is historic (more than two thousand years old) and worth overview, the focus of this section will pertain to the disruption of that relationship in the last fifty years – and the implications of events occurring in the first two decades of the third millennium.

In the modern Middle East, Islam is central to politics and identity. At the beginning of the last century, various Islamic reform movements began to reconcile Muslim religious and cultural life with Western values. Still ardently professing Islam as the central pillar of society, these movements indicated that doctrine was to be the basis of community formation: thus, non-Muslims would continue to be relegated to the status of *al-dhimmī*[1] and the validity of their role in state government remained tenuous. In some territories of the Ottoman Empire, however, Arab nationalism emerged as an ideological basis for political participation; Christian Arabs were attracted to this school of thought on the basis of shared language and cultural heritage, which led to the development and popularization of Pan-Arabism. As the concept of the

---

1. The term *al-dhimmī* is used in the Islamic world to describe the Christians and Jews with whom the Prophet Muhammad or later caliphs had a covenant. The term in Arabic means "covenant" and "security." For more details see Al-Kashf, *Miṣr al-Islamiyya*, 9–10.

nation-state spread throughout the region, the old system of political Islam[2] was redeveloped as Pan-Islamism: a system of belief that nationalism and doctrine played complimentary roles in the formation and administration of a modern nation-state.

In the second half of the twentieth century, Arab Christians faced distinct challenges as a result of their difficulty existing, let alone prospering, within the system of political Islam. They existed in an inherently authoritarian political system with access to limited democratic representation; civil society was weak, opposition to the government was subject to (and readily dealt with by) government authorities, and voices that advocated for human rights were under ready threat. Another challenge came from the very ideology of political Islam, a belief system with parties and proponents who actively sought to marginalize non-Muslims within the cultural and political milieus. The potential conflict between Islam and the West, therefore, acted to renew old hostilities between Muslims and Arab Christians. Colonialism, which resulted in the forced opening of the Arab world to Western culture, led to new weaknesses in national commitment and encouraged the emergence of regional and ethnic leaders who became involved in regular localized conflict.

Much assessment and analysis of the status of Arab Christians has been conducted in the last half-century. Some lend credence to the academic Samuel P. Huntington's popular theory of the clash of civilizations, which is pertinent particularly for Arab Christians as the scholar predicted that the next major global conflict would likely be of a religious nature. Others believe that recent military intervention in the Middle East by the West under the pretext of supporting religious freedom, human rights, and minorities has led many Muslims to reject this ascendant Western influence, viewing such a turn of events as the herald of a new era of Crusades. To counter this situation, Arab Christians have promoted the concepts of Arab nationalism, state nationalism, and citizenship, in order to establish grounds for political participation based on equality and freedom. Arab Christians maintain that Arabism should not replace religion. Despite statements made by the majority of Arab Christians

---

2. In the last three decades the term "political Islam" has been widely used in the writings that deal with the development of Islam as a political discourse. The term indicates all groups that consider Islam as a total religion. In the Arab world, ʿAshmawī claims that he is the first one that used the term political Islam in his book *Al-Islām al-Siyāsī*. For more details see ʿAshmāwī, *Al-Islām al-Siyāsī*, 244; See also Husayn, *Global Islamic Politics*; Roy, *Failure of Political Islam*; Sivan, *Radical Islam*; and Mussalli, *Moderate*.

that their commitment to the Middle East supersedes religious differences, they are still perceived to be alien to the greater Arab culture in some contexts.[3]

Although Arab Christians face a number of stark challenges, the development and contemporary conditions of today's Egyptian church, the consolidation of political Islam and Pan-Islamism, the potential impact of the clash of civilizations, and the danger posed to Arab Christians by Islamist governments loom among the most prescient and timely concerns facing populations of Arab Christians today and will be discussed further in this section. This chapter will also discuss additional matters related to the mid- to-late twentieth and early twenty-first centuries, including the consequential formation of the state of Israel and the comparatively recent events of the Arab Spring.

The Church in Egypt

By traditional accounts, Christianity was introduced to Egypt in the first century after Christ. It is recounted that St Mark, famed for the composition of his eponymous synoptic gospel, brought the message of Jesus and his faith to Egypt. The Copts believe that he engaged in his acts of Egyptian evangelism between the years of AD 40 and AD 68 – the apparent year of St Mark's martyrdom. The Coptic Orthodox Church, reportedly founded by St Mark in Alexandria (the same city in which he was martyred), has since grown to become the largest Christian denomination in the Middle East.

The Orthodox Church is generally referred to as the "Coptic Church" in the West; this nomenclature is descriptive of its Egyptian roots, rather than its Orthodox nature. The word "Copt," derived from the ancient Egyptian "Gypt,"[4] was used to describe the Egyptian population prior to the arrival of the Arabs in AD 642; after wresting control of the region from the Byzantine Empire, the name of this newly subjugated group was added to the dominant Arabic lexicon. At the time of the Arab conquest, the majority of Egypt's population – approximately 95 percent – were Christians. Shifting in meaning from its ancient origins, the "Coptic" identifier no longer referred to all Egyptians: in the parlance of the surging Islamic caliphate, the term came to refer only to those Egyptians who did not convert to Islam.

---

3. The only exception is Christians in Lebanon, where religious affiliation is the basis of rule, where the President of Lebanon is agreed to be Christian.

4. Meaning "Egyptian."

Over its two thousand years of history, the Orthodox Church has undergone few changes. The institution has preserved a number of traditions and practices that have existed from the beginning of the church's history, including the eminent role of the Coptic pope and the belief that consistent religious fasting (approximately two-thirds of the calendar year, if possible) brings a worshiper closer to God. Orthodox Christians fast every Wednesday and Friday, as well as during special fasting periods: the fifty-five days before Easter, the forty-three days prior to Christmas, fifteen days in reverence of the Fast of the Virgin, another three days for the Fast of Jonah, and additional non-fixed days for the Apostles' Fast – leading up to Apostles' Day, on July 12.

The ceremonial matters of the Orthodox Church have also been maintained throughout almost two millennia. Orthodox Christians believe in the transubstantiation of the communion elements – the bread and the wine – into the body and the blood of Christ. In order for a person to take Holy Communion in the Orthodox Church, that person must be formally baptized in the Orthodox tradition; they must have also fasted for a given period before the communion and must have confessed their sins to an Orthodox priest. Until the late nineteenth century, Orthodox mass was held in the Coptic language: the fourth stage of development of the ancient Egyptian tongue, expressed in Greek characters with four additional letters meant to emulate the sounds of the earlier hieroglyphic-based language. The gradual change in the language of the formal masses from Coptic to Arabic came as a result of the reality that, over time, most of the church's congregants no longer understood the Coptic language. As Coptic was supplanted by Arabic, Bibles were translated into the latter language; contemporary Orthodox masses are celebrated in the Arabic language, supplemented by some liturgical passages in the traditional Coptic.

The immensity of the Islamic influence on Egyptian society is witnessed in the fact that almost all modern Egyptians speak a dialect of Arabic and approximately 85 percent of the population is Muslim. In pre-Arab Spring government schools, much attention was paid to the matters of Islamic heritage and the Arabic legacy of Egypt. Egypt's historical Islamic eras and interactions with neighboring Muslim states dominate the public study of history, contributing to a degree of common identity with the Islamic *ummah*,[5] or nation. In working toward diplomacy and unity with other Arab-identifying states, former Egyptian President Gamal Abdel Nasser often emphasized this Pan-Islamic identity. His willingness to embrace the popular doctrine of Arab

---

5. Arabic term meaning "people" or "nation" and often used to refer to the greater Islamic population, regardless of national or ethnic identity.

socialism, when paired with his effective appeals to the *ummah*, contributed to his positive and charismatic reputation.

Other Egyptian politicians, however, struggled to engage fruitfully with the greater Arab sphere. Despite his efforts to establish a reasonable peace between rival Middle Eastern states, former President Muhammad Anwar el-Sadat received less support from the Egyptian citizenry than his predecessors. El-Sadat often spoke of the Egyptian identity as opposed to the wider Arab identity but found difficulty in publicly presenting himself as a pious Muslim. In order to bolster his religious credentials, the president began to refer to himself as the Ra'is al-Mu'mineen,[6] an honorific that displays the deep influence of Islamic civilization upon Egyptian society and its increasing relevance over the past seventy years.

Although much of the outside influence exerted upon Egypt came from the Islamic sphere, the nineteenth century was host to a different influence: Western churches, which engaged in missionary work in the Levant. In the century prior to these activities, the myriad churches of the West began to reason out which Middle Eastern nations would be the focus of their missionary activities; in short order, the United Presbyterian Church – an American denomination – began active missionary work in Egypt.

The Presbyterian missionaries employed traditional missional activities, including the establishment of service institutions such as hospitals and schools – facilities used to not only benefit the community but exemplify the Christian mission. A number of Orthodox Christians responded positively to the missionaries' system of faith, reflecting the discontent felt by attendants at Orthodox masses: faced with the church hierarchy and a Coptic liturgy incomprehensible to most congregants, some Copts (especially those possessing higher education) welcomed the Reformed theology introduced by the Presbyterians.

Over the last two centuries, the successor to these efforts – the Evangelical Church of Egypt[7] – has become the largest Protestant church in the Middle East. As of 2020, the Evangelical Church has over one million members worshiping in more than 440 churches. The Evangelical Church's Synod of the Nile consists of eight presbyteries from the Nile Delta to Aswan, with administrative headquarters in downtown Cairo. Organizationally, the denomination is similar to the Presbyterian system: it possesses a stated clerk, an elected

---

6. Arabic term meaning "president of the faithful" – a play on the early Islamic caliphal title Amir al-Mu'mineen, meaning "commander of the faithful."

7. In Egypt, we use the term "evangelical" to refer to Protestant churches.

moderator, and twelve councils responsible for different sectors of church activity. These councils are responsible for matters ranging from hospitals and medical services to the operation of the sixteen schools administered by the synod, as well as evangelism, financial affairs, service and development sectors, communicates and publishing, ministerial and governmental affairs, and so on.

It is also worth briefly discussing the Catholic presence in Egypt. For spiritual guidance, this population looks to the Coptic Catholic Church – an entity in communion with the Roman Catholic Church, notable for its continuing use of the Coptic language in its liturgy. Established via missionary action on the parts of the Capuchin and Jesuit religious orders in the seventeenth century, the group's numbers have ebbed and flowed over time. In the current era, the Coptic Catholic Church retains over two hundred local churches in Egypt; the entity also administers 170 schools, a reminder of the educational traditions held by the aforementioned Capuchins and Jesuits.

The Evangelical Church of Egypt was born, then, as a result of the missionary movement of the United Presbyterian Church. There are seventeen other Protestant denominations present in the country, representing the full range of contemporary Christianity: among them are the Assemblies of God, the Baptist Church, the Methodist Church, the Church of the Brethren, the Church of God, the Apostolic Church, the Pentecostal Church, the Church of Christ, and others. The combined population of these groups is above two million Egyptians – including Presbyterians – worshiping at approximately 1,500 local churches. These institutions also exist in Egypt as a result of successful missionary activities in the country, an effort that has certainly had a positive influence on the state of the church in Egypt. The introduction and popularization of Reformed theology – a system of faith and biblical assessment quite different from the preeminent Orthodox view – could be considered an Egyptian reformation due to the long-standing impact it has had upon the country's Christian community. This new movement also faced a counter-reformation conducted within the Coptic Orthodox Church: changes were made to better accommodate the uneasy congregations, such as shifting from the traditional use of Coptic in Orthodox masses to the more widely understood Arabic language.

Not all of the Western influences introduced to Egypt through missional efforts were necessarily positive, however. Reformed theology, although flourishing in the country, was formulated, of course, in Europe and the United States. In Egypt, however, adherence to Reformed theology meant a lack of local theological development: despite being structurally independent for decades, local churches continued to experience the theological suggestions of non-local church entities. A secondary effect of this dependency has been the popular societal association between Egyptian Protestant churches and the West; a place, from the Egyptian point of view, that is perceived as overly Western (meaning overly broad-minded, with a more progressive attitude that is totally different than eastern traditional churches).

As the two main Christian denominations in contemporary Egypt, the Orthodox and Protestant institutions face different issues with respect to their position in society. The Orthodox Church might be considered "conservative," as their theology and traditions have remained largely unchanged for approximately two thousand years. It places emphasis on tradition, ties to the original church, and its historical relationship to its founder (St Mark) and his personal relationship with Christ. Further focus on the lives of the saints and the acquisition of blessing through contact with them, in addition to the extensive monastic tradition retained within the Orthodox Church, has further contributed to the conservative nature of the establishment. The Protestant church, on the other hand, was born from the Western church: it has adopted liturgy and hymns utilized by its progenitors and has also focused on a social message that has reached a large number of Egyptians. One issue that united both the Orthodox and Protestant churches, however, was a mutual conclusion that each of their primary tasks was to proclaim the word of God. As a result, both groups respectively focused on evangelism among the existing Egyptian Christian population as the central ecclesiastical goal until the year 1950.

The institution of the church in Egypt has historically and traditionally focused on evangelism as the driving force of denominational activity, opting to hold a more pessimistic view of social ministry. This emphasis occurred as a result of several factors:

- The church has been in a position in which it is fighting to survive and has therefore not been able to fully participate in the life of the Egyptian community.
- Theologically, the church has focused on evangelism as an individual goal, as opposed to evangelism as part of – or partnered with – social ministry.
- The church has held the fundamental understanding of the gospel as an invitation to eternal life, rather than a call to enact social change.
- Social action was not considered a priority of the institutional church during the first half of the twentieth century.

Political Islam

Religion and politics are intricately intertwined in the Arab world. By the end of the twentieth century, the Islamic resurgence was the central feature of Arab politics. The impact of this ascendant religious influence can be seen in all aspects of Arab society, from the state of women's dress on the streets of Middle Eastern capitals to increased demands for faith-based institutional accommodations (Islamic laws, punishment, taxes, and financial institutions).[8] Political Islamic language dominates the voice of regional regimes through the consistent promotion of ideological values. From the streets and homes of Middle Eastern families to the halls of governmental power, political Islam has dramatically asserted itself in both the personal and the civic lives of Muslim communities.[9]

According to the beliefs of prominent Muslim scholars and leaders, there is no separation between politics and religion. Although its political cohesion was damaged early as a result of internal leadership conflicts, the Prophet Muhammad founded a religious state that his successors transformed into an empire. The elaboration and the application of the laws derived from the Qur'an and the Hadith – reports of the sayings and deeds of the Prophet – produced a remarkably homogeneous international society, bound by common customs and procedures that led to the creation of a distinct Islamic identity.[10]

In the Muslim world, there exist three major schools of thought related to the emerging forces of Islamic resurgence. Proponents of the first trend would prefer to align Muslim countries with the West. They promote the "progressive" values of the West in the name of "modernization" and opt for the secular principles that contributed to Western civilization as a basis for state and society. According to this view, religion should be limited to personal affairs and kept separate from matters of government.[11]

Proponents of the second trend believe that theological doctrine and political realism necessitate violent Islamic revolution. This emergent trend is described as "political Islam," and its proponents promote the belief that the West is the central antagonist of Islam and Muslim nations. According to this model, the Islamic system of governance is not an alternative but

---

8. Islam has a wide view of financial institutions and how they should be structured, including several kinds of taxes like Zakat, which is the financial contribution of every Muslim to help the poor in society.
9. Esposito, *Islam the Straight Path*, 156.
10. Ruthven, "Islamist Movement," 18.
11. Ahmed, "Islam and the West," 67–68.

an imperative inspired by, and inherently designed to accommodate, God's message as interpreted through Islamic scripture and Shari'ah (the Islamic legal system). Those promoting this belief system popularly state that all Muslims must obey and follow this divine mandate, and that those Muslims who do not adhere to Shari'ah are *kafir* (nonbelievers) and should be considered apostates from the Islamic community. *Jihad* (struggle) against unbelief and unbelievers is a religious duty within the framework of political Islam, and participants consider themselves members of the army of God in battle against the followers of Satan. These militants extend their opposition from "illegitimate" governments and peoples to the state-sanctioned *ulama*, government-aligned religious institutions, and the state-supported mosques. In their eyes, those following other Abrahamic faiths are unbelievers – rather than *ahl al-kitab*, "people of the book" – due to their corruptive connections with Western civilization, Christianity, and Zionism.[12]

The third trend, Islamic revivalism, emphasizes the role of Islam as a total and comprehensive way of life. Its adherents state that religion is integral to politics, law, and society, and that the failure of the Muslim community in the face of the West has come as a result of its departure from "true" Islam and modern preference for secularism. The renewal of Islamic communities requires a return to a more theologically pure interpretation of Islam: a religiopolitical and social reformation that draws its inspiration from the Qur'an, the life of the Prophet Muhammad, and the lives of those who participated in the early Muslim movement. To restore God's rule and to establish a true Islamic social order, as promoted by the Islamic revivalists, this divine law must replace Western civil codes; modernization is subordinate to Islamic belief and values, as science and technology are required specifically for developing Islamic society. Islamization (or re-Islamization) of the current political, economic, and social structures is the ultimate goal of this trend.[13]

We will now explore the ideologies of the second and the third trends in detail, and hope to illustrate the extensive impact made upon the Egyptian political system by the modern Islamic resurgence.

---

12. Ahmed, 63–64.
13. Esposito, *Islam the Straight Path*, 163.

The Ideology of Political Islam[14]

Modern Islamic militant groups drew great inspiration from *al-Ikhwan el-Muslimun*, an Egyptian Islamist organization better known in the West as the Muslim Brotherhood. Founded by Ḥassan al-Banna in 1928, this organization's power often waxed and waned within Egyptian borders; its ideology of instituting a uniquely Islamic state, however, found fertile ground in a newly emergent generation of international Islamic revolutionaries. These militants, emboldened by the global influence of their ideology, widely considered the surviving members of the Brotherhood as ineffective and "burned out."[15] Hoping to draw a line between themselves and that last generation of Islamists, modern militants have aimed to reinvent their movement and replace their less successful predecessors. Nonetheless, many leaders of modern Islamist groups base their ideology on the theories and works of Sayyid Quṭb, an Islamist author and member of the Muslim Brotherhood jailed and hung by the Nasser regime. Quṭb is considered by many to be the most influential Egyptian Islamist theorist: his widely read narrative, *Maʿālim fī El-Tarīq* (Milestones),[16] has been cited by a significant number of more recent Islamic authors as central to the continuing development of theocratic thought in the Islamic world. Although he drew from a number of influential figures, many of Quṭb's ideas were inspired by the Indian scholar Abul Aʿla Maududi (1906–1979) whose works were translated into Arabic during the 1950s.

The nationality sought by Islamist groups is one of doctrine: a wide ideology, where all nations become equal under the flag of God.[17] Quṭb emphasized an active faith, grounded in the belief in the unity and the sole authority of God, as the basis for Islamic community. He promoted the key concept of submission to God alone – not to any human authority – as expressed in the establishment of Shariʿah as the sole source of legislation for almost all aspects of human life. In accordance with his certitude of Shariʿah's centrality, Quṭb subsequently theorized that belief in the unity of God entails submission to his authority in both areas of worship and sovereignty. Hence, betrayals of that belief – either by worshiping other gods or submitting to sovereigns other than the divine – are to be considered unbelief.

---

14. Political Islam is a wide category that includes different topics of discussions related to the basic concepts of "Islam" and "politics." Islam is a religion that controls mundane life too. For this reason, Islamic revivalism is dealt with under political Islam.

15. Ibrahim, *Egypt's Islamic Militant*, 497.

16. Quṭb, *Maʿālim fī El-Tarīq*.

17. Quṭb, 26–29.

In *Ma'ālim fī El-Tarīq*, Quṭb posited that true freedom and justice manifest only through the Islamic "system." He argued that the Western hegemony was approaching its collapse: not because it was materially poor, but because science – the discipline that produced enlightenment, per Quṭb's theory – had proven incapable of promoting moral progress. As a result, the West was unable to provide the world with values capable of improving humanity's moral and ethical state. Per Quṭb, humanity stood on the brink of the abyss not because of the threat of annihilation hanging over its head (which was just a symptom of the disease, according to Quṭb, and not the disease itself) but because humanity had become bankrupt of those values which foster true human progress and development. Quṭb stated that even the West recognized the validity of this claim, as it had become patently obvious that the West could no longer provide the upright societal values necessary for humanity to prosper.[18]

As opposed to "soft" and corruptive philosophical sciences such as psychology, "hard" physical sciences – among them physics, medicine, the creation of art, and the development of technology – are not antithetical to Islamic progress; rather, per Quṭb's revivalist framework, embracing them should be considered an essential element of Islamic ascendancy. Quṭb argued that many prominent examples of "Western" science in fact originated in Islamic universities, only to be co-opted and twisted by European imperialists and secularists; conversely, the prominence of philosophical sciences in the secular West acted as an ongoing cornerstone of *jahili*[19] authority. Philosophy presumes that the meaning of human existence is a legitimate field of human inquiry, rather than a mystery known only to God, and renders the world devoid of divinity; all of the physical sciences, on the other hand, must be conducted in a manner that leads to Allah. According to Quṭb, this Islamic truth – that human existence is a mystery known only to God – is the core teaching of Islam and, when informed by a theologically inspired engagement with science, contains the answers to the basic questions of human existence: why we are born, for what purpose we live, and why we die.[20]

The political thought of Quṭb is based on the concept that Islam is not theory but practice. The first step in building the revivalist community is thus based on the Islamic call, "There is no God but Allah." As the nascent Islamic

---

18. Quṭb, 5.

19. Derived from the Islamic concept of *jahiliyya* (ignorance) and used to refer to the way of life and/or period of time that existed in Arabia before the revelations of the Islamic prophet Muhammad. This term is also used to refer to the secular and modern Western world by Islamist scholars such as Abul A'la Maududi.

20. Quṭb, *Ma'ālim fī El-Tarīq*, 138–145.

community is established and its needs are identified, a system of rules and regulations become possible to determine. Quṭb argued that preoccupation with specific institutions of government are no more than the misguided obsessions of the governing discourse. Those who ask Islam to provide a theory of the state seek to reduce Islam by insisting that it is cast in the same terms as man-made theories of sovereignty. According to Quṭb, those people do not know the nature of Islam and the basic call of that religion.[21]

Paramount among Quṭb's arguments is the necessity of participatory governance. He based this concept of government on a number of related Qur'anic passages that discuss the Islamic concept of *shura* (consultation). These passages encourage believers to settle their affairs by mutual consultation and advise believers to seek counsel from their brethren in all affairs. Within his framework, the details are left open to the Muslim society based on Islamic beliefs.[22] These matters – the type of consultation required, the identities of who should participate in such consultation, the timing of such consultation, and the format of such consultation – could thus be quite variable. Quṭb believed that, on the one hand, the ruler receives his power from the will of the governed; on the other hand, such power depends on the ruler's commitment to Islamic law rather than faithfulness to the governed.

Quṭb argued that the Islamic social system is not a historical system, existent in the past and now relegated to memory. Per the author, the Islamic social system is a live one – and by his estimate, it is a futuristic system. According to Quṭb, the Islamic system is not a local system, it is a universal one; the only system that can meet humanity's needs.[23] The Islamic system came from the Islamic religion, a universal faith; subsequently, it is not a system for one period of history or for one generation. It is a fixed system provided by God to renovate human life.[24]

Quṭb believed that the social system and the doctrine of Islam are intimately bound together. The social system emerged as a result of doctrine, and all the characteristics of the system are based on the means by which a society interprets Islam. Divine religion can't be restricted to people's hearts, worship, and personal matters, according to Quṭb: divine religion must include the whole range of human activities and direct all aspects of life. There is no separation between the faith mandated for eternal life and the faith utilized

---

21. Quṭb, 39.
22. Quṭb, *Ma'raikat al-Islam wa al-Ra'smalya*, 70.
23. Quṭb, *Naḥwa Mojatam' Islami*, 17.
24. Quṭb, *Al-Mostaqable le-Haza al-Din*, 10.

by human beings in regard to earthly matters. The divine religion is essential, both "here" and "there."[25]

Quṭb declared Islam to be the solution for all our basic problems. The faith and its accompanying system provide a comprehensive model of social justice: Islam restores justice to its followers in their dealings with the state: justice in money, justice in chances for societal success, and justice in matters of governmental judgment. By Quṭb's estimation, Islam is an ideal framework for Egypt – more so than any other, in fact, and deserving of authority.[26] Quṭb acknowledges that Islam allows private property but goes on to argue that, since such ownership is conceived of as mere stewardship of common property, the right of the Islamic government to redistribute such property as it sees fit is an appropriate counterbalance to the concept of earthly property ownership.

Quṭb predicted that the Cold War rivalry between capitalism and communism would end and that the next global conflict would be between communism and Islam. For Quṭb, communism represents a firmly materialistic idea while Islam represents a humanistic one. The author had no doubt that Islam would be victorious in this ideological conflict.[27] We can summarize the main themes in Quṭb's thought as follows:

- The world today lives in *jahiliyya* (ignorance) – a state similar to the spiritual and social disregard of the Arabs prior to the revelation of the Prophet Muhammad.
- One must believe in God's sovereignty – not in human sovereignty – and proclaim God alone as the divine lord of both this world and the realm of eternal life.
- One must prepare for a comprehensive revolution against earthly human sovereignty, in all its aspects and systems.
- One must reject all human made systems such as democracy, authoritarianism, capitalism, and communism. In all of these systems, the human egregiously supplants God as sovereign.
- One must encourage people to live their lives as led by the Islamic religious calling, even if they already profess Islam. Muslims do not need to believe in, or live within, any other framework – national, social, or economic.

---

25. Quṭb, 12.
26. Quṭb, *Ma'rikat al-Islam wa al-Raasmalya*, 36.
27. Quṭb, *Nahwa Mojatama' Islamy*, 39–40.

- The sovereignty of God cannot coexist with human sovereignty, just as good cannot cohabit with evil. The only way for either of these forces to survive is by destroying the other.
- Islam is the solution for all of life's basic problems, both earthly and spiritual.
- Future conflict will be conducted between Islam and the West (in this case, Quṭb assumes that communism will represent the West).

These are the main themes in Quṭb's writings. He was convinced that a grand effort was necessary to restore Muslims to their divine religion and to implement the divine law in order to reestablish Islamic society. This plan could be summarized as follows:

- To break with *jahili* society, and to reject that society by not participating in it.
- To reject all books – including Islamic hermeneutics – and focus only on the book of God, the Qur'an.
- To ignore the requests of unbelievers for an ecumenical program of rule and focus on the Islamic calling. After all, Islamic rule is based on the establishment of a firmly Islamic society; the political reality will develop according to the needs of that society.
- Restoration of Islamic society and establishment of the kingdom of God will not be accomplished through speeches and oration, but by power, action, and the sword.
- *Jihad* (struggle) is the basis for the Islamic calling. When Muslims stop engaging in the practice of *Jihad*, Muslims stop engaging in the practice of Islam.

Modern Islamic militants ascribe to many themes derived from the works of Sayyid Quṭb. The slogans of such groups, including phrases like "Islam is the solution," are derived from his concept of rejecting any political program or agenda before establishing a pure Islamic society. As a result, it is easy for current militant groups to promote this slogan without taking any responsibility for developing a realistic political program.

Quṭb also promoted the practice of Muslims accusing other Muslims of *takfeer* (disbelief). In discussing the matter, the author ponders the subject of a Muslim prison guard harshly punishing his prisoners – men who are members of the Muslim Brotherhood, a fact known to the prison guard. Within Quṭb's framework, this prison guard is not a legitimate Muslim: he knowingly acts against those fulfilling the divine will and does so in support of a non-Islamic state. Quṭb also processed the personage of the prison's president: this figure lends direction and authority to the oppressive guard, and receives the same type of support from the director of prisons, the state director of security, and the supervising minister of state. Thus, the circle of disbelief extended to the leaders of the country, including President Gamal Abdel Nasser himself. As the president of a country directs the currents of national culture, Quṭb extended his circle of disbelief to include the entirety of Egyptian society. Per Hamooda's estimate, the circle of disbelief and its population of disbelievers were in a constant state of expansion.[28]

Quṭb borrowed terms such as *jahiliyya* and *takfeer* from El-Maududi, doing so without any consideration of the Indian cultural and religious background of such a figure. By my estimate, Quṭb's concept of Islamic society is similar to that of Jewish society: both of them are based on religious identity, rather than national identity.[29]

Both Quṭb and Samuel Huntington agree about the decline of Western culture, as well as the global rise of non-Western civilizations; they also agree about future conflict between Islam and the West. One difference between Quṭb and Huntington lies in their predictions about future conflict: as stated earlier, Quṭb assumes communism (representing materialistic Western culture) will destroy capitalism, only to be in turn defeated by Islam. Huntington and Quṭb also disagree sincerely about the role of Islam: Huntington sees Islam as a source of conflict; Quṭb considers Islam as the only system of faith by which humanity can find a place for peace and justice. Additionally, Huntington criticizes the idea of international civilization, whereas Quṭb argues that Islam must be an international religion to succeed.

I believe it is clear that the intent of political Islam in all its forms is to establish an Islamic state. The application of the Islamic law and creation of a global Islamic *ummah* – either by using armed force to enact regime change or via a societal process of Islamization – acts as a rallying call for those people mobilized to act in the establishment of an Islamic state. Quṭb's ideas – his use of *takfeer*, the contemporary prevalence of *jahiliyya*, and the necessity of humanity's role in implementing the Islamic state – continue to act as major inspirations for modern political Islamists.

The Challenge of the State of Israel

Since the establishment of the state of Israel in 1948, Arab Christians have struggled with the religious aspect of the Jewish state – a crucial issue in modern geopolitics. One could argue that the establishment of such a polity

---

28. Ḥamooda, *Sayyid Quṭb*, 132.
29. Diab, *Sayyid Quṭb*, 106.

contributed to a blurring of the lines between religion and politics, justifying this century's militant Islamists as they move forward in their efforts to establish an Islamic state.

Another result of the establishment of the modern state of Israel was the violence that swept the region. Many people in both the West and Middle East began to see parallels between the foundation of contemporary Israel and events in the Old Testament; this led to a view of the Old Testament as a "book of violence" by some Christians, and the God of the Old Testament as a deity promoting war crimes and legitimizing murder for the sake of his chosen people. In some cases, the theological adjacency of the text to modern Israel has resulted in the marginalization of the Old Testament among Christians in the Middle East.

For Arab Christians, it became necessary to differentiate between the Old Testament manifestation of Israel and the modern state of the same name. In the Middle Eastern context, the doctrine of "land and covenant" became a core component of contemporary theological assessment. The matter of covenant is considered a major issue in the Bible: many believe that Reformed systems of thought effectively depend upon covenant theology as a basis for further interpretative assessment. Many false concepts of the covenant between God and his people have emerged in recent years, especially the concepts related to God's covenant with the people of Israel, as well as the covenantal relationship to the church and the condition of the current state of Israel. Speaking broadly, the concept of covenant is not limited to these issues but extends to all aspects of contemporary life.

There are a number of different covenants in the Bible, from the Old Testament to the New Testament. These include the covenants of Adam, Abraham, Noah, Moses, King David, and lastly, the covenant between God and the church mediated through Jesus. Within this subject, the relation between the covenant and the law is important – as is the relation between the Jews and the land of Palestine. Here, Arab theologians believe that the immigration of the ethnic Jewish people to Palestine during the last century was not based on fulfilling the covenants of the Old Testament; in contrast, Middle Eastern Christian theologians view this movement of Jews to the land of Palestine as lacking viable theological value.[30]

Along these lines, we can explore the position of the late Pope Shinoda (1923–2012) – a prominent church leader who dealt with the presence of Israel in a unique way. One could argue that the most important issue addressed by

---

30. Zaki, "Middle Eastern," 557–558.

Pope Shinoda concerned the state of Arabs within Israel. Approaching the issue from political and theological perspectives, he argued that the modern Jewish people are not the chosen people of God, and that Palestine is not equivalent to the biblical promised land. He believed that God allowed the Jewish people to inhabit Palestine in a pagan age – a time when the worship of idols was commonly practiced.

According to Pope Shinoda, God intended to save his faithful from pagan oppression. Through his prophets (at that time, followers of the Jewish faith), God called his faithful to defensively separate themselves from the pagan nations. After doing so and going on to form the nascent state of biblical Israel, the Jewish people began to mix with other nations – in direct opposition to God's directives – and the worship of foreign idols spread among them. Since the days of ancient Israel, the covenant of God has been carried forward into Christianity, a faith meant not for any specific ethnic or national group but for each and every person in the world. As a result, there is no longer any reason for separation from other peoples, and there is no longer any promised land.

The Pope disagreed with the claim that the foundation of the modern state of Israel is the fulfillment of Old Testament prophecies regarding the return of the Jewish people to the "Promised Land." Pope Shinoda declared that these prophecies were already fulfilled, when the Jews returned to the land after their exile in Babylon, and that the promise of God would not be fulfilled again. Shinoda believed that the Jews who now occupy Palestinian land are doing so under the authority of Lord Balfour's promise,[31] rather than God's promise.[32]

Pope Shinoda forbade Coptic pilgrimage to Jerusalem, and denounced Copts who travelled to the city. Hundreds of Copts were required to apologize publicly in the newspaper for the sin of visiting the Holy Land against his wishes. Shinoda argued that the Holy City was under Israeli occupation and that religious visits there by Copts should be postponed until they could go in the equal company of their Arab kin.[33] Shinoda believed that, by going to Jerusalem, Copts betrayed Arab interests and disregarded the severity of the Palestinian affair.[34] He claimed that the Holy City was not established by the Jews, that their rule over Jerusalem was meant to last for a limited time, and

---

31. In 1917, Lord Balfour, United Kingdom's minister of foreign affairs, promised the territory of the Palestinians to allied Jews (to be governed independently as their own country) as part of the First Balfour Declaration.

32. *Al-Muṣawar*, 5 January 1996, 28–29.

33. *Waṭanī*, 18 October 1998.

34. *Rūz al-Yūsif*, 18 October 1996, 13.

that all the archaeological excavations underway there were being conducted in an attempt to legitimize Israeli authority over the Holy City.[35] The pope affirmed in many interviews and discussions that Jerusalem should be under Arab control and that it was imperative that Jerusalem be freed from Israeli occupation.[36]

One can argue generally that Arab theologians agree on the contemporary and political realities of modern Israel, including its contested prophetic role as derived from Old Testament theology. They argue that, within the Christian framework, the covenant between God and Abraham now reaches further than the authority of one nation-state, and beyond geographical boundaries as defined by humankind. In fact, the church itself is the new Israel and its authority extends well beyond geography and ethnicity.

From our study of political Islam and an overview of the challenges that have emerged as a result of the foundation of modern Israel, one can also conclude that, during the second half of the twentieth century, Christians in Egypt were subjected to the impact of political Islam in all its forms. Militant groups killed Christians, burnt their churches and homes, and generated a great deal of fear among the Copts; additionally, the re-Islamization of Egyptian society – as led by groups such as the Muslim Brotherhood – created new and distinct challenges. Political Islam had begun to truly push the Copts to the margins of society via the authoritarian tools of social alienation and fear.

The redevelopment of political Islam and the emergence of the state of Israel were not the only factors that put new pressure on Middle Eastern Christians. As assessed in Huntington's clash of civilizations theory, another element contributing to discontinuity was the potential of future conflict between Islam with the West. This prediction created a new challenge for Arab Christians, who were labeled as a fifth column within Middle Eastern society for their faith status and their apparent religious relationship with the West. Although the Egyptian Christian community has always stated clearly that their commitment is to the nation and peoples of Egypt, and that their culture is deeply intertwined with Arabism, suspicions regarding their connection with the "Christian West" acted as a point of conflict that pushed Copts further from the cultural mainline.

---

35. *Al-Ahrām*, 8 October 1998.

36. In every interview with Pope Shinoda, his position on the relationship with Israel (as well as visits by pilgrims to the Holy Land) was stable and consistent. The pope had been invited to many panels in Egypt and other Arab countries to present his opinion about Jerusalem and the position of the Copts with regard to the occupied city.

The Clash of Civilization

Samuel P. Huntington (1927–2008) predicted that the future composition of the world would be based on dominant cultural entities, and that conflicts would emerge based on cultural conflicts between each of these civilizations. According to Huntington, cultural identity is paramount to most people; it supersedes ideological, political, and economic identifiers. The great conflicts to come will not be between social classes – the rich and poor – but between those peoples having drastically different sets of values and traditions. Central to Huntington's thesis are the "fault lines between civilizations": world regions where dangerous cultural conflicts have emerged historically and where they continue to do so. Huntington observed that nation-states have begun to increasingly define their interests in terms of their cultural identity, allying with other powers belonging to the same civilization. To support this presumption, the author argued that, in 1993, nearly half of the forty-eight ongoing ethnic conflicts in the world were between groups of different cultural origins.[37]

For Huntington, religion is the most important element defining civilization. By his assessment, religion is the central force that motivates and mobilizes people, and the means by which a society engages in its religious life largely determines the characteristics of its governing bodies. The separation of spiritual and temporal authority in the West led to the prevailing of cultural dualism; in the contrasting East, the separation between religion and state was prevalent only in the Dharmic civilization, among those peoples who practiced Hinduism, Jainism, and Buddhism. In Islam, God is Caesar; by the Taoic standards of China and Japan, Caesar is God.[38] Huntington observed that, as economic and social modernization grew to become global in scope, a worldwide revival of religion occurred simultaneously.[39] The religious resurgence involved people returning to, and giving new meaning to, the traditional religions of their communities. In some cases, these faith efforts were accompanied by the militant purification of religious doctrine and the reshaping of personal, social, and public behaviors in accordance with religious tenants.[40]

Within the Islamic structure, religion became the source of personal identity, meaning, and hope. The faith was also an essential source of governmental stability, legitimacy, and power. Keeping in mind the tenants

---

37. Huntington, *Clash of Civilizations*, 20–37.
38. Huntington, 64–70.
39. Huntington, 95.
40. Huntington, 96.

of the clash of civilizations, the slogan "Islam is the solution" is stated in opposition to the solutions offered by dualistic Western culture and religion. According to Huntington, however, there is an analogy to be made between the Islamic resurgence and the Protestant Reformation. He writes:

> Both are reactions to the stagnation and corruption of existing institutions; advocate a return to a purer and more demanding form of their religion; preach work, order, and discipline; and appeal to emerging, dynamic, middle-class people. Both are also complex movements, with diverse stands, but two major ones, Lutheranism and Calvinism, Shi'ite and Sunni fundamentalism, and even parallels between John Calvin and the Ayatollah Khomeini and the monastic discipline they tried to impose on their societies. The central spirit of both the Reformation and the Resurgence is fundamental reform.[41]

Huntington argues that the sweep of democratization in the 1970s and 1980s had little to no impact on the Muslim World. While democratic movements were gaining strength and coming to power in the various countries of Europe, Latin America, and East Asia, Islamist movements were gaining strength in Muslim countries. These groups dominated local power structures, moving from the offices of the opposition party to the halls of governmental power in rapid fashion. After acting to clamp down on any opponents to their rule once in power, Islamist movements induced their tethered governments to promote Islamic institutions and practices while also incorporating Islamic symbology and phrasing into governmental systems. These trends coincided with the "oil boom" of the 1970s and an upswing in the population rates of Muslim nations. The result of these factors is a large and restive population of young people who believe themselves to be protagonists for protest and reform, governmental and societal instability, and – inevitability – revolution as a basis for Islamic revival.[42]

According to Huntington, peoples and counties with similar cultures are coming together while peoples and countries of different cultures have begun to come apart. Power blocs defined by ideology and "great power" politics are giving way to political alignments defined by culture and civilization. Political boundaries are increasingly redrawn to coincide with cultural ones: ethnic, religious, and cultural matters are becoming the central lines of conflict in

---

41. Huntington, 111.
42. Huntington, 114–120.

global politics.⁴³ In the post-Cold War world, countries relate to civilization in the following ways:⁴⁴

- *A cultural nation-state*: a country that entirely identifies with one civilization.
- *The core state of the civilization*: that is, its most powerful and culturally central state (or states). The core state(s) is the source (or sources) of the civilization's culture.
- *The lone nation-state*: an entity which lacks cultural commonality with other societies.
- *The cleft countries*: entities that territorially bestride the fault lines between civilizations. These states face particular problems in the maintenance of their unity.
- *The torn counties*: a state that succeeds in redefining its civilizational identity. There are three requirements to achieve this goal: the support of the political and economic elite, the willingness of the public to acquiesce to the redefinition of their general identity, and the willingness of the dominant local civilization to embrace this cultural conversion.

Huntington concludes that the process of identity redefinition would be painful, interrupted, and that – as of the date of his writing in 1996 – all attempts had failed. For him, the core state is the most important one in the fault-line conflict, and when – as in the Islamic context – a core state is absent, major internal and external conflicts tend to occur. This absence becomes a source of internal strife and an external threat to other civilizations.⁴⁵

Huntington disapproves of the Western concept of "universal civilization" as an evolving and uniting concept. Per Huntington, the belief that opposing societies could be brought together through new commonalities – coexistence in neutral cities, adherence to globally popular languages, or the influence of assumptions, values, and doctrines (often held by those in the West) – is an irrelevant and unrealistic one. Huntington believes that the eighteenth-century concept of "universal civilization," which suggests the eventual emergence of a singular enlightened society, was likely generated as a response to the Western anthropological obsession with "primitive" peoples. In more recent times, says

---

43. Huntington, 125.
44. These descriptions drawn from Huntington, 125–140.
45. Huntington, 135–177.

Huntington, the concept of a "universal civilization" could be applied only to the elite classes in both Western and non-Western civilizations.

Some European and American voices claim that the "Christian West" does not have problems with Islam, only with violent Islamist extremists. This does not deny, however, that the fortunes of the two religions have risen and fallen over the centuries in a sequence of momentous surges, pauses, and counteractions. According to Huntington, Islam is the only civilization that has put the survival of the West in doubt. The scholar argues that the nature of the two religions, as well as the civilizations based upon them, are the likely causes of this ongoing pattern of worldwide issues. Modern conflict is a product of differences: the Islamic concept of religion – a way of life that transcends and unites religion and politics – versus the Western Christian ideals that separate the realm of Caesar from the realm of God. The conflict has also stemmed, however, from their similarities: both are monotheistic religions and see the world in dualistic "us vs. them" terms, whereas polytheistic religions assimilate additional deities and values with relative ease. Both are universalistic, claiming to be the one true faith to which all humans can adhere. Both are missionary religions, believing that their adherents have an obligation to convert non-believers to that one true faith.

In the 1980s and 1990s, the overall trend in Islam shifted toward an anti-Western direction. This has entailed emphasizing and exaggerating the differences between Islamic and Western civilization; proclaiming the superiority of Islamic culture; and promoting the need to maintain religio-cultural integrity in the face of Western onslaught. Radical Muslims see Western culture as materialistic, corrupt, and immoral. Secularism and non-Islamic religiosity – and, hence, immorality – are worse evils than the Western Christianity that produced them. In the Cold War, the West labeled its opponent as adhering to "godless communism"; in the post-Cold War clash of civilizations, Muslims see their opponent as "the foodless West."[46]

To emphasize his points regarding a ramp-up in contemporary intercultural conflicts, Huntington presents figures that demonstrate the high rates of intergroup violence enacted by twentieth-century Muslims in comparison to peoples of other civilizations. Per the author, there are a number of explanations behind the matter of violence between Muslims and non-Muslims, as well as the issue of intra-Islamic violence. These causes are as follows:[47]

---

46. Huntington, 213–214.
47. Huntington, 213–214.

- The expansion of Islam brought its practitioners into direct contact with many different peoples, most of whom were conquered and/or converted; the legacy of this process remained.
- The existence of non-Muslims in Islamic societies, as well as the existence of Muslims in non-Islamic societies, acts as a possible source of conflict. As mentioned earlier, Islam loosens the boundaries between religion and politics – and in doing so, draws a sharp line between those living in the Dar al-Salam (the abode of peace) and the Dar al-Ḥarb (the abode of war).[48] As a result, Huntington believes that practitioners of different religions are better equipped to live with one another within a multi-religious society than within an Islamic society.
- The absence of a core nation-state has allowed Islam to act as an unchecked source of instability in the world, as the faith lacks a powerful center.
- The population growth among Muslims – especially among unemployed males – contributes to instability and civil violence, both within Islam and against non-Muslims.

Huntington argues that, despite the decline of the West and the emergence of other civilizations, the West is different from any other civilization that has existed, inaugurating worldwide processes such as modernization and industrialization.[49] While acknowledged the question of the decline or renewal of the West as a valid matter of debate, Huntington suggests that the assessment of that "decline" includes matters such as crime, drug use, violence, family decay, a general weakening of work ethic, a rise of the cult of personal indulgence, a decreasing commitment to learning, and decline in "social capital" – that is, membership in voluntary associations.[50]

It is clear to Huntington that the renewal of the West is possible. To achieve this goal, he believes that the United States and European countries must work toward the following objectives:

- Achieve greater political, economic, and military integration among Western powers.

---

48. Dar al-Salaam (the abode of peace) and the Dar al-Ḥarb (the abode of war) are references to traditional Islamic division of the world. The lands inhabited and governed by Muslims is the abode of peace, and the lands of non-Muslims is the abode of war. These terminologies reflect where Muslims can enact war, and where they cannot.
49. Huntington, 262–265.
50. Huntington, 302–304.

- Incorporate the Western states of Central Europe into the European Union and NATO.
- Encourage the "westernization" of Latin America.
- Restrain the military development of Islamic and Sunni countries.
- Slow or halt Japan's shift toward China-friendly policies and developments, in order to better bring the county and its culture back into the "Western" sphere.
- Accept Russia as the core state of Orthodox Christianity and acknowledge it as a major regional power in the post-Soviet era.
- Maintain the superiority of Western technology and military over other civilizations.
- Decrease Western intervention in the affairs of other civilizations, as these actions could contribute to instability and potential global conflict in a multi-civilizational world.[51]

Arabic Views on the Clash of Civilizations

I believe that Huntington was correct in his declaration that economic modernization and religious resurgence went hand in hand at the end of the twentieth century. Many of the trends in the world contradict the enlightened belief that modernity and secularism are one, and this belief is further contradicted by many of the trends in the world today. However, I also believe that Huntington's assumptions regarding international conflict based on the clash of civilizations overly simplifies the complex context of international relations.

In the Arab World, journalists and writers responded readily to Huntington's thesis. "Nothing new with Huntington," declared an article by A'bed-Alla Ben A'lly Ala'lyan, who claimed that Huntington's ideas were popularized to better meet the needs of Western institutions – many of which, he states, are preferential toward a world busy with conflict. Ben A'lly Ala'lyan maintained that Huntington's beliefs regarding the alignment of Islamic civilizations and potential cooperation between Muslim societies is not a solid theory, and that Huntington's fear of non-Western civilizational development seems to reflect the West's desire for superiority – although Western civilization suffers from distinct and observable spiritual and moral decline. A'bed-Alla Ben A'lly Ala'lyan disregarded Huntington's thesis as having been produced to satisfy policy makers in the West, and concluded that one should recall the conflicts

---

51. Huntington, 311–312.

of the past before attempting to promote dialogue and understanding between civilizations.[52]

Some writers attributed Huntington's work to cultural ignorance, bigotry, or other sinister intentions. Mona Mo'nes, an educated Egyptian woman, considered Huntington's clash of civilizations a theory informed by racism. According to Mo'nes, the information about Islam in Huntington's work was taken from secondary sources only and was thus inaccurate; she goes on to state that the apparent objective of the scholar's work was to discredit the Islamic civilization and downplay any future achievements.[53]

Another critique came from the well-known philosopher Fo'ad Zakaria, who argued that Huntington's ideas were the cultural products of the American Central Intelligence Agency (CIA). Observing connections between Francis Fukuyama's concept of the end of history and Huntington's clash of civilizations,[54] Zakaria argues that the conflicts discussed by Huntington were conducted in an earlier stage in the history of humankind and that humanity survived this period of conflict in order to prosper in the modern era. According to Fo'ad Zakaria, conflict is possible even in societies with values like freedom and social justice. When these important issues are neglected, the old conflict – that clash of civilizations – rears its ugly head. As a result, Zakaria views Huntington's work as a fabricated study published to promote Western superiority and assist in the stabilization of its economy, which had begun to falter in the face of non-Western civilizational ascendance.[55] The clash of civilizations is the conflict between religions and more specifically a conflict between Islam and the West. He went on to critique the idea of the singular West, arguing that all cultures learn from one another. According to Zakaria, the history of civilizational development was based upon shared exchange and transmission.[56]

In the introduction to the 1998 Arabic edition of *The Clash of Civilizations*, Salaḥ Qonṣwa rejects Huntington's attribution of a unique quality to Western civilization. Qonṣwa argues that Huntington has confused the causes of events with the results of those events, including an overt focus on the "historical moment" as a formative force contributing to the special quality of the West. According to Qonṣwa, this "historical moment" was not a *cause* of Western

---

52. Ala'lyan, "Ṣdam El Ḥadarat," 86.
53. Mo'nes, "Miṣr fe 'oyon el Gharab," 50–51.
54. The "end of history" suggests that the victory of liberal democracy over communism would be the end of ideological conflict, and that liberal democracy is thus the only legitimate and final form of government.
55. Zakaria, "Thaqaft el Mokhabarat," 22.
56. Zakaria, "Ḥadaratna wa Mafhom el-Sera," 26.

ascendancy: it was a concept that was produced as a *result* of Western hegemony. Huntington neglected to consider that the causes which led to Western ascendancy could have led to the same result in another place or with another civilization. He criticizes Huntington's theory of historical conflict, stating that his view – that conflict started between rulers and then nations, and then evolved into conflicts between ideologies and entire civilizations – was deeply inaccurate. Qonṣwa references the events of World War II in support of this claim: Italian Catholics fought against French Catholics, evidence that contemporary global conflict would not just occur between those of opposing faiths.[57]

Qonṣwa drew a sharp distinction between "culture" and "civilization." For him, culture consists of two opposing dimensions: the spiritual and the material. The spiritual dimension includes customs, values, systems, and beliefs; the material dimension encompasses both physical and immaterial ideology, in terms of buildings and tools. Qonṣwa's culture is not static and, as evidenced by history, societies can consist of multiple contradictory cultures. In the Middle Ages, civilizations (the material side of culture) were composed of distinct societies, and each society could be assessed within its extant culture. In the modern age civilizations act as a currency exchanged between societies and have become more independent from culture. Culture gradually became restricted to the spiritual dimension, and civilizations began to encompass multiple societies. Civilizations began to separate from their cultural roots; over time, it became less arduous for societies to maintain the material sphere (civilization) while the spiritual sphere (culture) became independent under the contemporary alias of "culture." Qonṣwa argues that different societies and nations can participate in one universal civilization, but only if they are open to change and willing to learn from one other.[58]

Huntington is right to note that the individualistic values enshrined by Western liberal democracy do not command universal assent and are not authoritative for all cultures. From this perspective, Huntington rejects the idea that Western values are universal – but his theory that fault-lines between civilizations are the source of war is a misunderstanding of the present, and

---

57. Qonṣwa, introduction to *Clash of Civilizations*, Arab ed., 16–17.

58. Qonṣwa concludes that Huntington set out a new map for the management of world conflict resolution, and that the clash of civilizations was the result of a new political agenda derived from current and relevant economic and political situations. See Qonṣwa, introduction to *Clash of Civilizations*, Arab ed., 20–21.

a mistaken diagnosis of both the potential for tragedy and the opportunities for cooperation that our present circumstances entail.⁵⁹

Now, as in the past, wars are commonly conducted between (and within) states and societal groups, and not between different civilizations. Whether or not they act as the agents of nation-states, the familiar pragmatisms of territorial sovereignty, self-determination, and politically expedient alliances often impel members of the same "civilization" to strife against one another while making common cause with those of different "civilizations." This can be observed in the historical example of the Armenia-Azerbaijan conflict: Iran threw in its lot with its geopolitical allies in Christian Armenia, and not with its spiritual kin in Islamic Azerbaijan. The kaleidoscope of shifting alliances in the Balkans tells us a similar story. To this end, it is evident that some of this century's most infamous and decisive conflicts have been "inter-civilizational." The Iran-Iraq War and the genocide of the Tutsis by their Hutu neighbors occurred within what Huntington understands as single civilizations. World War I is commonly, and not inaptly, described as a European civil war; the Korean War and the Vietnam War were conflicts among states that justified their claims by references to "Western ideologies." Huntington's typology of civilizations does not map on to the history of twentieth-century conflict.⁶⁰

Political philosopher and former professor of European thought at the London School of Economics, John Gray, posits that it is not right to take for granted that capitalist economies everywhere produce individualistic values. The capitalisms of East Asia are not the products of individualist culture, for instance: thus, different religions and cultures can produce different market economies. Contrary to Huntington, Gray argues that in the economic rivalries of the coming century, cultural differences will be central, and the emergence of genuine market economics will force the interaction among cultures as an inevitability of the market.⁶¹

It is quite clear that the clash of civilizations became central to the agenda of policymakers, theologians, sociologists, journalists, religious institutions, and academic discourses. Huntington was right about the emerging role of civilizations, but to indicate inter-civilizational conflict as the deciding factor in the future order of the world is, I believe, inaccurate.

I believe that cross-civilizational concerns contribute to world order and disorder, but I am sure that they are not the only source of conflict. To

---

59. Gray, *False Dawn*, 165.
60. Gray, 156–157.
61. Gray, 158.

replace Islam with communism as the potential enemy of the West is unfair and destructive. Communism was, after all, a product of the West, whereas Islam is an Eastern religion rooted in the Arabic culture. I believe that, in this multicultural and ever-changing world, the West does not need a monolithic enemy. Dialogue and mutual understanding are basic requirements for this coming century.

Nowadays we see the rise and fall of independent market economies in East Asia, a trend of Eastern spiritual and cultural movements spreading rapidly in the West, and extensive cultural interactions between spheres in the areas of arts, athletics, and culinary matters. Universal civilization is the only civilization which emerges from equal interaction between different cultures. In my estimation, a universal civilization encompassing different cultures is a source of hope for future peace and integrity. This universal civilization should not be a construct of Western preference, but rather a great society capable of accommodating universal principles from all different civilizations.

"Universal civilization" does not mean the absence of cultural identity; to the contrary, a legitimate universal civilization will recall cultural identity and affirm its peoples' roots and cultural commitments. A universal civilization would allow different cultures to interact and exchange ideas, values, and spiritual trends, resulting in a new understanding of each culture. I agree with Huntington in regard to his theory of "cultural restructuring," a system in which peoples originally identified by their religion may shift into an identity of nationality. Cultural assertiveness is required in a universal civilization, but what is not needed is for culture to become the only source of identity – and thus, a primary source of conflict. To ensure that culture is not the only source of identity, we must be clear about the term "universal." According to Huntington, universalism is an ideology employed by the West during its confrontations with non-Western cultures; this supposition by Huntington is only accurate if we conclude that the "universal civilization" is a Western one.

While I disagree with much of Huntington's basis for the *Clash of Civilizations*, this does not mean I believe that the entirety of his work is to be disregarded as inapplicable to contemporary matters. In my opinion, Huntington's concept of religious resurgence is very relevant to the modern-day Middle East. In most of the countries of the region, the element of Islamization was essential for its development, economics, and politics. Keeping in mind the relatively recent events of the Arab Spring, the popular political reaction to Islamization and authoritarianism could be observed as a counterweight to the phenomenon of religious resurgence.

The Arab Spring

By 11 February 2011, Egypt became the second Arab country (after Tunisia) to join the spring of revolutions which seemed to sweep across North Africa, ousting its political regimes and shaking the prevalent structures of power. From Tunisia and Egypt, these winds of change swept toward other Arab countries and pushed the entire geopolitical region into a state of transition. Yemen, Bahrain, Libya, Syria, Jordan, Algeria, and other nearby nations found themselves swept up, the citizens of their nations having eagerly awaited a gale of freedom. The entire world carefully watched these events, live and in real-time.

The December 17 self-immolation of a Tunisian vendor named Mohamed Bouazizi did not only spark the 2010 revolution in Tunisia (which ended with the capitulation of its long-time president Zine El Abidine Ben Ali), this act triggered widespread turmoil across the Middle East. His protest regarding confiscation of goods, police harassment, and personal humiliation led to the start of some of the most pivotal extra-national protests and uprisings of the modern age.

Egyptian youth, many of whom had already planned to participate in widespread protests scheduled for 25 January 2011, found themselves inspired by the Tunisian experience and increased their demands: only the removal of the entire Egyptian political regime would suffice. Eighteen days of televised protests, sit-ins, and more active forms of disobedience were enough for this young generation of Egyptian protesters to oust the Mubarak regime and dissolve its state security apparatus.

As the Tunisian experience inspired the Egyptian protesters, the events in Egypt inspired those in other Arab countries to rise up against their dictatorial and brutal political regimes. From the gulf to the ocean, many Arab rulers came to understand that the status quo – one that had existed in their countries for years, even decades – was no longer acceptable to a large percentage of their population, particularly among the youth. At the time, citizens of Arab nations hoped that these changes would lead to stable democratic transitions at the political, economic, societal, and cultural levels. A dramatic juncture had been reached by the Arab citizenry and the authorities, including those retreating from power and those coming into power.

The January 25 Revolution

The January 25 Revolution indisputably reversed the state of affairs in Egypt. Among the most important revolutions of our time, this popular act by the

Egyptian people triggered radical changes at many different levels of society. At the political level, the previous regime – in all its corruption, tyranny, and despotism – collapsed. At the time, it was believed that Egypt had begun a new age of democracy. At the economic level, Egypt became a fertile ground for investors. State-allied capitalists who had previously monopolized the national economy departed, and – against all expectations – the Egyptian stock market swiftly overcame concerns of collapse. At the social level, Egyptian youth popularly expressed their wish to unite and develop their communities regardless of religious, ethnic, or cultural affiliations. Egyptian youth had shown ability to demand their rights and confront corruption in all its forms despite great risks. At the cultural level, many sensed a unifying atmosphere of cultural awareness thundering throughout Egypt.

The revolution riveted the Egyptian (and global) public, causing citizens of all age groups to follow the news – whether printed independently, broadcast on the radio, or displayed on the screens of televisions and smartphones. In the immediate post-revolutionary period, the bond between the people and the media seemed to have strengthened. For the first time, the Egyptian public engaged freely with media figures and resources.

Although the Egyptian revolution was focused on national rather than religious concerns, one of its unanticipated outcomes has been an increase in religious tension between Muslims and Christians. Despite cooperation during anti-regime protests, sporadic – and then more consistent – conflict between the groups has led to political uncertainty concerning the concept of a civil state and the formation of a widely recognized constitution.

In the immediate post-revolutionary context, the concerns were as follows:

- *Religious tensions*: The downfall of the former regime allowed for the unleashing/untethering of pent-up religious animosity. Radical Islamists began to act against Christians, in both material forms (physical assault and murder) and spiritual forms (church arson and hate speech).
- *Economic crisis*: Despite a positive economic outlook after the revolution, Egypt's currency has since lost a third of its value. Ongoing regional geopolitical concerns related to food and water security only worsened these concerns.
- *Absence of security*: Since the retreat of the police and the retraction of their authority in January of 2011, and despite all efforts to return order back to the streets, the general issue of public security became an issue that has impacted daily life across the country.

- *Emergence of Islamist movements*: After the regime's downfall, Islamist groups – including Salafi organizations and the Muslim Brotherhood – stepped forward to lay out their agendas and fill the political power vacuum.
- *Popular demands on foreign policy*: After decades of frustration in regard to an Egyptian foreign policy regarded as corrupt and non-representative of popular views, the Egyptians "on the street" began to call for open participation in the matter of diplomacy.

In the context of new developments in the Middle East, a reflection on the impact of Islamism is a difficult task due to the unexpected revolution. However, there are certain issues that contributed to these developments – and went on to become much more grand concerns only a few short months later.

Islamists in Power

Explicit revolutionary accusations were directed against specific religious movements: many protesters stated that groups such as the Muslim Brotherhood did not support the Arab revolutions until after they succeeded and that, in Egypt, they derided protesters while supporting the former regime. Despite these concerns, the currents of Islamism won popular support – and new power at the inaugural ballot box – as a result of post-Arab Spring democratic exercises. In Egypt, Libya, and Tunisia, Islamists were able to rise to power with general ease.

In Egypt, popular elections were held to select who would hold the reins of power in the revolutionarily dissolved People's Assembly and Shura Council, as well as the presidency itself. Subsequently, Islamist movements – among them the aforementioned Muslim Brotherhood and Salafist cadres – gained approximately 70 percent of the seats in the Egyptian parliament.[62] Concerns were voiced among nascent liberal and civil groups, along with Coptic Christians, in regard to the near-total control of the Islamist movements over the new government and its role in creating a new constitution; similar alarms were raised upon the ascent of Islamist figures to power in Tunisia. It should be noted, however, that each country's post-revolutionary political scene was influenced by separate matters: Islamist movements in these countries are not at one shared level of political consciousness or militancy, as the social and political environment in either place determines the level of a group's political awareness and activity.

---

62. 'Abd el 'Aziz, "Lemaza Yafoz Al-Isalmyyon?"

It can be concluded that the Arab Spring was transformed into an Islamic Spring,⁶³ as represented by the swearing-in of the Islamists to the halls of power. Some in Egypt proposed that the benefit of the doubt be given to these religiously motivated entities, as they had no previous opportunity to exercise their political rights after decades of repression and brutality under the previous regime. It was hoped that the involvement of these movements in national political and social life would limit and reduce the degree of their religious intransigence. Others agreed, calling for a realistic approach in dealing with these organizations. Their adherence to post-revolution voting initiatives, and their popular support, acted as pragmatic reminders along the democratic path of least resistance.

Religious Tensions

The end of the Mubarak regime seemed to open the floodgates of hard-line Egyptian religious currents. These influences manifested in the political arena and were reinforced by an unusual wave of militancy. After the revolution, Egypt witnessed a significant number of sectarian and religious incidents, such as:

- *The incident of the burning of the Church of the Two Martyrs 2011*: On March 5, 2011, a church attack occurred in the village of Soul in Atfiḥ, and its contents were stolen. After that, some individuals attacked Coptic houses in the village and also destroyed some parts of the church.⁶⁴
- *Coptic ear cut off*: In March 2011, a group of Salafis cut off the ear of a young Christian in Qena, Upper Egypt, in an apparent application of Shariʿah.⁶⁵
- *The attack on the Copts of Abu Qurqas 2011*: On 19 April 2011, an attack took place on the Copts of the village of Abu Qurqas in Minya Governorate in Upper Egypt.⁶⁶
- *The 2011 Imbaba church attacks*: On 7 May 2011, a series of attacks took place in Egypt against Coptic Christian churches in the poor working-class neighborhood of Imbaba in Giza, near Cairo.⁶⁷

---

63. El Feqi, "Bal Hwa Rabe"; see also Dorgham, "Makhawf."
64. *Al-Ahram*, 5 March 2011.
65. *El Nabaʾ*, 6 January 2017.
66. *El-Marsry El-Youm*, 20 April 2011.
67. *El-Youm El Sabeʾ*, 7 May 2011.

- *The Maspero massacre*: This initially started as demonstrations in October 2011 by a group dominated by Egyptian Copts in reaction to the demolition of a church in Upper Egypt claimed to be built without the appropriate license. The peaceful protesters who intended to stage a sit-in in front of the Maspero television building were attacked in October 2011, resulting in 24 deaths, mostly among the Coptic protesters, and 212 injuries, most of which were sustained by Copts.[68]
- *Dahshur incident*: In August 2012, a fight broke out in the village of Dahshur that devolved into Molotov-laden civil unrest. The events resulted in the injury of two officers and thirteen recruits, as well as the destruction of four stores owned by Copts.[69]
- *Forty-two Coptic churches attacked and destroyed after July 2013*: During the presidency of the former President Mohamed Morsi, he isolated himself from his people while he was still in power and did not share politics with other parties. After his fall, the Egyptian authorities dispersed the sit-ins of the Muslim Brotherhood supporters in Raba'a Al-Ad'awiya Square and the Nahdat Miṣr Square in August of that year.[70]

Political and Social Marginalization

The prominent roles of women and young people in the revolution were seemingly disregarded, as these groups were marginalized from participating in the creation of a new Egypt. Copts, too, were disinvited from these historic decisions despite their proud identification and behaviors as Egyptian citizens – and not just as Coptic Christians – throughout the revolution. This phenomenon manifested clearly in the parliamentary elections, held from 28 November 2011 to 11 January 2012. The victors were mostly outwardly religious characters, and many Egyptians voted based upon their religious affiliation.

Some described the Egyptian Christian community's "coming out from behind their church's walls" – doing so after decades of socio-cultural isolation – as an act of rebellion against the representation of the Coptic Church and their political leadership. These behaviors were also described as a victory for the role of the secular Egyptian citizen which developed at the sit-ins of Tahrir Square and state institutions. These individuals and groups claimed their rights

---

68. *BBC*, 9 October 2011.
69. *El-Youm El-Sabe'*, 30 December 2012.
70. *BBC News Arabic*, 11 August 2018.

publicly and did so without the permission or safeguarding of their religious authorities. The negative events, political marginalization, and sectarian tensions experienced by Christians after the revolution, however, seemed to suggest the potential for a rapid relapse into oppression; subsequently, some Christians returned to the material and spiritual protection of their churches.

Outcomes

The Egyptian assessment of the consequences of the January 25 Revolution were regarded as both positive and negative. The constructive results included the building of solidarity between Christians and Muslims in their efforts to remove the dictatorial regime, as well as a general societal shift toward a state that functioned by legal (and not dictatorial) mechanisms. However, no one can deny the negative outcomes of the revolution: a rolling economic crisis that eventually sapped over 50 percent of the Egyptian pound's value, an increase in religious tensions, a long-term lack of security that varied from place to place, a muddled approach to foreign policy, and general governmental disorganization. Many of the positive and negative outcomes were anticipated, as Egyptians were familiar with the events that had occurred in other places experiencing revolution. The most unexpected outcome, though, was the rise of the Muslim Brotherhood to power and the institution of Islamist policy via the apparatus of the Egyptian government.

In general, the Brotherhood's regime was not so different from any other: the economic crisis continued, religious tensions increased, and security forces did not engage proactively with safety concerns. The combination of these qualities, however, spelled trouble for the Copts. The biblical imperative to "love your enemy" became largely impossible in this new Coptic context, and thousands of Christian worshipers went to their churches to pray for divine rescue. New difficulties bled in, even in those holy places: a radical attack upon St Mark's Coptic Orthodox Cathedral in Cairo, the residency of the Coptic pope, acted as a sign that there were no more uncrossable "red lines." Few Copts migrated out of Egypt for security purposes, however, instead opting to work alongside moderate Muslim populations to remove the Muslim Brotherhood from their new position of authority.

The June 30 Revolution

After years of sporadic attacks on Coptic individuals and institutions, the June 30 Revolution was a remarkable moment in the existence of the Coptic Christians and Egyptians in general. As Islamist radicals burnt churches,

Coptic leaders affirmed their commitment to the nation of Egypt and rejected any foreign military interference enacted to protect them. As a result, a new Coptic reputation – enthusiastic in its loyalty to the nation – was introduced to the Muslim Egyptian public.

No one could fathom the speed with which the Muslim Brotherhood came to power in Egypt – nor the expediency with which they were removed from power. The *ikhwan*[71] understood themselves to be the "people of God," believing that divine support allowed them to replace Mubarak's corrupted regime. Additionally, they benefited from popular support, expansive financial resources, international figures who reinforced the group's efforts, and the support of affiliated *ikhwani* militants. In that context, their influence was absolute: people, power, money, and religious influence were well within their wheelhouse. With such a strong start, some leaders of the Brotherhood spoke of the possibility of their group ruling Egypt for the next five hundred years.

In short order, however, Egyptians – both Muslims and Christians – were back on the streets with the purpose of enacting early elections. This goal was based on a number of factors, as follows:

- The fear of losing the pan-religious Egyptian identity to a decidedly more religious identity.
- The replacement of the primacy of the state with adherence to the Islamic *ummah* – an entity that does not often recognize the borders between Islamic nations.
- The intermingling of religion and politics, which led to the popular belief that religion was being misused to further the agenda of the Brotherhood.
- Christian groups began to feel strongly that they were, at best, second-class citizens under the Muslim Brotherhood's new order.
- Ongoing compromise between the Egyptian state and regional terrorist groups.
- A general increase in religious tension, paired with the emergent influence of Brotherhood-linked religious leaders turned political figures.
- A new social coalition that emerged to oppose the Brotherhood, representing a majority of the population (including moderate Muslims and Christians).

---

71. Arabic word meaning "brothers" – a short-hand term referring to members of the Muslim Brotherhood.

- The tendency of the Brotherhood to enforce religious matters harshly regarding all aspects of Egyptian existence, greatly complicating the personal lives of Egyptians.
- The Brotherhood's increasing control over all aspects of Egyptian political life, ranging from the presidency to a majority within the parliament.
- Corrupt acts and practices employed by some of the Brotherhood's representatives and leading figures.

Millions of Egyptians joined the new protests, expressing a great desire to remove the Muslim Brotherhood from the halls of power. When they were denied the privilege of an early election, the public requested that the armed forces act to remove the Brotherhood from power on their behalf. The army responded, and 30 June 2013 saw the dawn of another era of Egyptian history.

Christians were recognized for their sacrifices during this new revolution, and for their strong participation in protest efforts. For the first time in the modern history of Egypt, Christians began to feel as if they could take part in governmental society. A new period of cross-cultural communication and civil participation was initiated, and the Copts began the process of restoring themselves as full participants within the Egyptian state.

One can conclude that the elements of discontinuity and continuity of Christian engagement with society in Egypt have been remarkable in their recurring nature over the last fifty years. One cannot deny that these two elements, the continuity and discontinuity, were neither diminished nor replaced by one another, but the continuing development of the Egyptian state – especially post-June 30, 2013 – has been very important to Coptic security and national identity.

2

The Church and the Kingdom of God

Social Responsibility

The kingdom of God rests at the heart of Jesus's message. From an exploration of the documented life of Jesus and his ministry, I hope to arrive at a holistic understanding of the kingdom and how it might shape our mission.

The question of whether to prioritize evangelism or social and political engagement has challenged the Christian church for nearly two thousand years. This question becomes more focused and intensely discussed when people query which is more important: to expend earthly currency and effort to support or change public structures in an effort to temporarily relieve the weight of the poor and suffering or to focus on the eternal salvation of one's soul? Is salvation for this life only or for the next life as well? Or, to put it another way, is salvation meant for the human body in the "here and now" or eternally in the kingdom to come?

There have been many works written to address this issue, including sections of this book. Some of these attempts focus on the basis of the biblical concept of salvation and social action, while others build from an analysis of a historical assessment and definition of oppression. Others approach the matter from a "middle ground" via a situational analysis paired with supportive biblical concepts.

While I do not reject any of the aforementioned approaches, my belief is that the most fruitful manner in which to engage with the question of evangelism is through the complex lens of Jesus's teachings and actions. This framework has developed out of my concern for the continuing role of the historical Christ – specifically, that there was a real person whose name was Jesus, that he lived his life among us, and that the account of his ministry was authentically recorded in the Gospels. The life and works of Jesus have great capacity to continue to teach his followers what their goals as Christians ought to be, and to better enable us to design our vocation and ministry accordingly. The teachings of Jesus are rich in meaning and substance: parables, proverbs, and commentaries on the law are included and are meant to be directly applicable to our Christian lives.

In this chapter, I will elaborate upon my study regarding the kingdom of God. I will show what I believe the kingdom meant for Jesus and how it became central to his teachings and actions. An assessment of how the kingdom will arrive – either as a present and terrestrial event or an eternal future reality – is my primary query within this portion of the text, and from this discussion I will develop my theory of the "kingdom of God" and how it shapes our view regarding salvation and social action. Through the theological lenses of the late Rev. Dr. Samuel Habib, I will also discuss at length an Egyptian perspective on the manifestation of the kingdom of God.

The Kingdom of God in Modern Interpretations

In recent times, numerous interpretations of the kingdom have been suggested. Most of these interpretations can be divided into the futuristic view and the present eschatological view. According to this framework, the future eschatological view emphasizes the future aspect of the kingdom while the present eschatological view emphasizes the present – and hence, social – nature of the kingdom. In the dominant present interpretation, the German theologian Albrecht Ritschl (1822–1889) acts as the most influential theologian to introduce to us the social concept of the kingdom. By his measure, the kingdom of God is "the organization of humanity through actions inspired by love"[1] and "the moral unification of the human race, through action prompted by universal love to our neighbor."[2] He goes on, stating that the kingdom is "the association of men for reciprocal and common action from the motive of love."[3]

Ritschl's views of a present eschatological kingdom of God inspired many other theologians of the nineteenth century. Some later figures, including

---

1. Ritschl, *Christian Doctrine*, 12.
2. Ritschl, 280.
3. Ritschl, 290.

church historian Adolph von Harnack and American Baptist pastor Walter Rauschenbusch, were profoundly influenced by Ritschl's method and theology. These men went on to reinterpret his theory on the kingdom, and both identified the necessity of active mortal engagement with this imminent manifestation of God.

For von Harnack, the kingdom of God is "the rule of the holy God in the hearts of individuals, the power that works inwardly."[4] He expressed the belief that the kingdom of God arrives on earth on a personal and individual basis, "by entering into [the Christian's] soul and laying hold of it."[5] He reduced the kingdom of God to the subjective realm, and understood it in clear terms as a relationship between the human spirit and God – participatory and working in the present.[6]

Rauschenbusch, conversely, was the prophet of the "social gospel" – the direct application of Christian ethics to the ills of the world, and the living out of the Lord's Prayer on earth. For him, the kingdom was to come to the earth in due time – an inevitable future, guaranteed by the work of the biblical Christ. Per the estimate of Rauschenbusch, Jesus "never transferred the Kingdom hope from Earth to Heaven."[7] In his 1912 work, *Christianity: The Social Order*, Rauschenbusch bluntly addressed the territoriality of the heavenly state: "The Kingdom is so much of this Earth that Jesus expected to return to Earth from Heaven in order to set it up."[8] For Rauschenbusch, the kingdom of God is always present and future – always coming, always pressing in on the present and inviting immediate action.

From the works of Ritschl, von Harnack, and Rauschenbusch, we can sense several unifying beliefs regarding the theory of the present eschatological kingdom. Every human life can share with God in the creation of the kingdom: a more noble social order best summarized as humanity organized according to the will of God. Their works imply the existence of the kingdom as the progressive reign of love in human affairs. Through his social ministry, Christ – and, subsequently, his fellow adherents to the school of present eschatology – discovered the importance of the doctrine of the kingdom of God, which bridged the gap between the religious and the social.

---

4. Harnack, *What Is Christianity?*, 60.
5. Harnack, 60.
6. Ladd, *Gospel of the Kingdom*, 16.
7. Rauschenbusch, *Christianity*, 49–66.
8. Rauschenbusch, 49–66.

A new type of interpretation of the kingdom of God was proclaimed, on the other hand, by church figures such as the German exegete Johannes Weiss and the Lutheran polymath Albert Schweitzer. This interpretation called for a consistent, "thoroughgoing," and solely futuristic eschatological view of the kingdom as an eternal and heavenly expression of God's message. According to this viewpoint, the belief that the kingdom was an ongoing process on earth "was to import an element which was not in Jesus' mind."[9] Via eventual cataclysmic means, the kingdom would only arrive at the end of the earth: a "miraculous intrusion of God . . . to terminate human history and inaugurate the Kingdom."[10]

Weiss believed that as Jesus did not provide any documented explanation for the kingdom of God, this meant that he assumed that his audience would understand him correctly without need for such an explanation. He went on to summarize Jesus's teachings about the kingdom of God in six points:

1. "It is radically transcendent and supramundane."[11]
2. "It is radically future and in no way present."[12]
3. "Jesus was not the founder or inaugurator of this Kingdom, but He waited for God to bring it."[13]
4. "The Kingdom is in no way identified with Jesus' circle of disciples."[14]
5. "The Kingdom does not come gradually by growth, or development."[15]
6. "The ethics that the Kingdom sponsors are negative and world-denying."[16]

Schweitzer agreed with Weiss on most of these points. He was convinced that Jesus posited, both directly and by the vehicle of his parables, that the kingdom would arrive by its own means and on a divinely mandated schedule. "Perhaps [he] expected the coming of the Kingdom at harvest time," pondered Schweitzer, and the inaccuracy of this prediction led to new consequences for Christ: a "change in his understanding" regarding the state of the kingdom,

---

9. Ladd, *Crucial Questions*, 29.
10. Ladd, 29.
11. Weiss, *Jesus' Proclamation*, 133.
12. Weiss, 133.
13. Weiss, 78.
14. Weiss, 75.
15. Weiss, 73.
16. Weiss, 134.

which – in order to best assist in its manifestation – "compelled [him] to suffer and die."[17] Kin to Weiss, Schweitzer identified the kingdom to be an "apocalyptic realm" ushered in by the hand of God and beginning "when history would be broken off and a new heavenly order of existence begun."[18] As identified by George E. Ladd, Schweitzer was adamant in his eschatological beliefs: Ladd summarized Schweitzer's belief in the heavenly state as "altogether future and supernatural."[19]

A third eschatological school of kingdom thought soon opened its doors: known as "realized eschatology," this theory was argued prominently by the British theologian C. H. Dodd. In *The Parables of the Kingdom* and other writings, Dodd suggested that the kingdom of God was present and active in Jesus's time – and that it was also to come in the near or foreseeable future. According to Dodd, Jesus did not understand the kingdom as an event or era: rather, it was "an order beyond space and time."[20]

For Dodd, the concept of the kingdom was clear to Jesus. He writes:

> Jesus declares that this ultimate, the Kingdom of God, has come into history, and he takes upon himself the eschatological role of the "son of man." The absolute, the Wholly Other has interred into time and space. And as the Kingdom of God has come and the Son of Man has come, so also judgment and blessedness have come into human experience.[21]

Dodd based his theory on biblical commentaries regarding the subject of the kingdom – in particular, Matthew 12:28 and Luke 11:20 – and argued that Jesus's fundamental proclamation was that the time had already been fulfilled, and the kingdom of God was already at hand (Mark 1:5). By this standard, one could infer that Dodd meant that the kingdom had already arrived in Jesus himself. The author handled the passages indicating the future coming of the kingdom of God by attributing such text to the early church and the apostles on the basis "that the earliest tradition of Jesus' teaching is characterized by realized eschatology."[22]

---

17. Hinson, *Integrity of the Church*, 60.
18. Ladd, *Gospel of the Kingdom*, 15.
19. Ladd, 15.
20. Dodd, *Parables of the Kingdom*, 42.
21. Dodd, 107.
22. Willis, *Kingdom of God*, 20.

Another type of eschatology to be assessed, "inaugurated eschatology," was introduced by George Kummel. He began with an analysis of terms used to describe the chronological status of the kingdom: "near," "to be at hand". He concluded that the word "near" inferred that "an event would happen soon, by which it is presumed that there would not be a long time to wait before it happened."[23] He reinforced this point by showing that Jesus employed a number of statements which, presumably or expressly, mentioned not the imminence but the eventuality of the kingdom of God. Kummel continued his analysis of certain words, moving on to the eschatological "day" – "the day of judgment," "that day," and so on. Kummel believed that, in these phrases about the eschatological day, "the Kingdom of God is expected as a future reality in Jesus message."[24]

Kummel presents Jesus as having expected the eschatological kingdom to arrive within a generation, but also as seeing the kingdom as a reality present in his own person. Jesus expected that he would be the judge in God's terrestrial domain; but since he was already among men, their reaction to him – the earthly Christ – would be the basis for their judgment by the eschatological Jesus of the future. The kingdom was thus already at work in his person, his acts, and his preaching. Accepting Jesus meant, in effect, that one was accepting the future kingdom. The kingdom had begun, and in him it would be consummated.

For Rudolf Bultmann and his works regarding the demythologizing of faith, "the gap between the Jesus of history and the preaching of the later church was not harmless, it was to be preferred."[25] In Bultmann's teaching, Jesus is present in the *kerygma* – a term that meant several different things in Bultmann's work, including:

- the preaching of the early Christian community
- the faith understanding of Paul or of the Fourth Evangelist
- the preaching that occurs in contemporary churches[26]

Bultmann concludes in stating that "Jesus viewed the Kingdom of God as an entirely future, world-transforming event. For Him, the kingdom is present in

---

23. Willis, 40.
24. Willis, 40.
25. Willis, 27.
26. Willis, 27.

the recurrent now of decision which people can experience in the demand for radical obedience as they continue to encounter their neighbors."[27]

When we come to review the conservative evangelical reaction to the kingdom, we encounter different perspectives. Per George Eldon Ladd,

> the Kingdom of God is the redemptive reign of God dynamically active to establish his rule among men. And that this kingdom which will appear as an apocalyptic act at the end of the age, has already come into human history in the person and mission of Jesus to overcome evil, to deliver men from its power, and to bring them into the blessings of God's reign. The Kingdom of God involves two great moments: fulfillment within history, and consummation at the end of history.[28]

According to the works of Ladd, the reign of God is not only in the human heart: it is in the act of the person of Jesus and in human history. From this we understand how the kingdom is both present and, at the same time, future. Ladd went on, speaking of two distinct ages: this age and the age to come. To solve the problem of how the kingdom is both present and future, he believed that the solution lay in the "dynamic meaning" of the kingdom of God. He understood it as the reign of God not in the eschatological framework, but as the dynamic presence of God's present reign. For Ladd, this meant that "God is no longer waiting for men to submit to His reign but has taken the initiative and has invaded history in a new and unexpected way."[29]

Ladd believed that the kingdom is a dynamic concept of the acting of God.[30] He supported this idea of the dynamic kingdom with an exegesis of Matthew 12:28; per his assessment, this portion of Scripture showed that God's dynamic reign incurred upon the present age "without transforming it into the age to come."[31] The author conducts an exegesis of other passages, including Luke 10:18 and Matthew 11:12, believing that those writings most effectively support his viewpoint of a multifaceted and ever-present divine state. Ladd presents God's love and judgment in the parable of Luke 15 to emphasize the importance of both salvation and judgment as central to the identity of this new kingdom.

---

27. Willis, 30–32.
28. Ladd, *Presence of the Future*, 218.
29. Willis, *Kingdom of God*, 48–49.
30. Ladd, *Presence of the Future*, 218.
31. Ladd, 149.

Ladd concludes his thoughts on the "dynamic kingdom" with these words:

> The kingdom is altogether God's deed and not man's work; it is neither the ideal good, nor inevitable progress, nor history, nor merely God working in history, but it is God's supernatural breaking into history in the person of Jesus. The coming of the kingdom into history as well as its eschatological consummation is miracle – God's deed.[32]

Ronald J. Sider presents a different and unique perspective on the kingdom, emphasizing the need for both evangelism and social concern. For Sider, contemporary charismatic and social activist groups interpret the kingdom according to their own narrow theology and thus miss the overall picture. He states that "it is surely striking that social activists, charismatics, and advocates of world evangelization often refer to the Kingdom and sometimes even cite the same texts to support their different (frequently one-sided) concern."[33]

Sider, in his book *One-Side Christianity?*, points out the biblical principles of the kingdom. He is convinced that Mark's Gospel presents the best summary of the kingdom: "After John was put in prison, Jesus went into Galilee, proclaiming the good news of God. 'The time has come,' he said. 'The kingdom of God has come near. Repent and believe the good news!'" (Mark 1:14–15). But what is the "good news" of the kingdom? According to Sider, "Jesus's response to John the Baptist demonstrates that Jesus viewed His preaching and healing as signs of the Kingdom."[34] Sider elaborates upon his understanding of what Jesus meant by the kingdom of God via what he refers to as the recounting of the prophets' messianic hope. For Sider, the prophets foresaw a future day when God's Messiah would come to pour out the Spirit in a brand-new way (Joel 2:28–29) and restore God's people as a visible and protected community living in right relationship with God, neighbor, and earth:

> In the midst of oppression, idolatry and captivity, the prophets looked to the future messianic time. In that day, in the power of the spirit, the Messiah would bring transformed relationships with God, neighbor and earth. There would be a new society genuinely living according to God's righteous laws finally inscribed on people's hearts and wills.[35]

---

32. Ladd, 188–189.
33. Sider, *One-Sided Christianity?*, 50.
34. Sider, 52.
35. Sider, 54.

In accordance with this passage, Sider found himself convinced that the gospel writers used different portions of the Old Testament to declare that Jesus was to be the fulfillment of these breathtaking messianic prophecies. Sider argues that, when Jesus preached his central message – the kingdom of God is near, repent and believe the good news – he meant two things: that the long-expected Messiah was coming near, and that the messianic age was breaking through to the present time. On the chronological matter of the kingdom as present or future, Sider is convinced:

> The kingdom which Jesus announced then had broken decisively into history in the person and work of Jesus the Messiah. But it would come in its fullness only at the return of the Son of Man on the clouds of heaven (Matthew 24:30). On that day, people will come from East and west to celebrate the messianic banquet in the final kingdom (Matthew 8:11).[36]

From the above statement, we can conclude that Sider is sure that not only is the kingdom of God a present reality, but it is also an eschatological event. For him, the kingdom is both the salvific proclamation of the word of God and the present healing of the sick and the oppressed. The kingdom, therefore, includes both salvation and social action. He writes: "Jesus, the kingdom, and all the blessings of the Kingdom are inseparable. One cannot have the ethics of the Kingdom or the forgiveness of the Kingdom apart from Jesus."[37]

Based on the information addressed in the previous passages, I believe that it is inadequate to argue that the kingdom of God is only an organization of humanity, or that the kingdom of God comes through the human action of love alone. In the present eschatological interpretation, the kingdom is a present entity – men and women looking for their brothers and sisters (particularly the oppressed) and acting to transform their situation. Here there is no room for the apocalyptic elements, and the kingdom is fulfilled only by human action. I believe that these theologians disregard the transcendent role of God and apply the kingdom only to the mere human situation. In the eschatological interpretation, the kingdom was transferred to another world: a dream in the mind of Jesus that the kingdom would come through his earthly life. This did not happen, and the dream was transferred by the early church to the eschaton – an eventual moment in our future.

---

36. Sider, 56.
37. Sider, 59.

I join with Sider in believing that the kingdom was a present reality coming into the world through the person of Jesus Christ. The Old Testament Scriptures quoted by Jesus indicate that the kingdom is here – now, and in our midst. According to Sider, several events from the Gospels support the view that Jesus considered the messianic kingdom to be present already. The passage that Jesus quoted from Isaiah (61:1–2) is widely accepted as a messianic passage, for instance. Concerning the source of his power over demons, Jesus declared: "if it is by the Spirit of God that I drive out demons, then the Kingdom of God has come upon you" (Matt 12:28).

I believe that, from these words of Christ, we can conclude that the kingdom is truly present and among us. In apparent agreement, Sider points out:

> Jesus knew that the Kingdom had not yet reached its culmination. The parables that talk of growth demonstrate that the Kingdom grows slowly now. Only in the future, will the harvest (a symbol of consummation) arrive (Mark 4:3–8). Sin and evil continue to flourish, so Jesus looked ahead to a time of eschatological fulfillment when, at the close of the age, the Kingdom would come in its fullness (e.g. Luke 21:27).[38]

The kingdom of God is both an ongoing event and a future hope. It is the supernatural action of God and it is also human action. I believe that it is clear from the quote that Sider regards the kingdom as a present reality, as well as a future one. For him, the kingdom contains two basic elements: the proclamation of the word of God for salvation, and social action – namely, the physical healing of the sick and the freeing of those in captivity. Sider is convinced that both are necessary for the kingdom of God to be fully realized. Thus, the kingdom of God exists both now and will exist again – a present reality and a future hope. It is the supernatural action of the divine, and it is also human action.

The kingdom of God doesn't belong exclusively to this age, though, as determined by its chronological primacy or its values and principles. It also belongs to that age which is to come. The kingdom of heaven – the realm of the Father – was incarnated in Jesus, and in his person he brings the future into the present: the age to come into this age. In the same way, the kingdom of God brings to us the age to come in this age. In this kingdom, Jesus invades human history and our hearts, bringing us a foretaste of the age to come.

---

38. Sider, 56.

In *The Mind of Jesus*, William Barclay analyzes the Lord's Prayer and concludes that "the kingdom is a state of things on earth in which God's will is as perfectly done as it is in heaven."[39] It is quite clear to me that the concept of the kingdom of God must be central to our understanding to the mission of the church, but that we must delve deeper beyond the concept of heavenly restoration when we assess this important subject. Frank Thielman analyzes this matter at length:

> When Isaiah spoke of God's restoration of His people, he sometimes used language similar to the language Mark uses to summarize Jesus' preaching. Isaiah 52:7–10 summarizes the deliverance of God's people from the Babylonians, which has been the prophet's focus since 40:1. In 52:7 he depicts a messenger who announces the "good news" (LXX, Evangelizomenou) that Zion's God "reigns" (LXX, Basileusei). In Isaiah, God can also speak of the imminent restoration of His people as "bringing my righteousness near" (LXX, Engisa; Isaiah 46:13; cf. 51:5; 56:1). Mark seems to have Jesus' proclamation of the kingdom's nearness in these terms. Jesus announced that the time of waiting for Isaiah's prophesied restoration had been completed – God's reign had drawn near in Jesus' preaching.[40]

C. C. Caragounis assesses Christ's dynamic take of the kingdom as follows:

> Jesus' conception of the Kingdom of God had continuity with the OT promise as well as shared certain features with apocalyptic Judaism, particularly Daniel, but went beyond them in certain important respects: (1) the Kingdom of God was primarily dynamic rather than a geographical entity; (2) it was connected with the destiny of the Son of man; (3) entrance into it was not based on the covenant or confined to Jewish participation and (4) whereas in apocalypticism it was a vague future hope. In Jesus it is definite and imminent; in fact, it demands immediate response.[41]

One could argue that connecting the concept of divine restoration to the apocalyptic Jesus confirms clearly the connection between the present and

---

39. Barclay, *Mind of Jesus*, 60.
40. Thielman, *Theology*, 66.
41. Caragounis, "Kingdom of God/Heaven," 420.

the future: again, that the kingdom is a current effort and future hope. In that context, Jesus of Nazareth not only brings the kingdom – he *is* the kingdom, in himself.[42] In Jesus's understanding of the kingdom, the reality of the "here and now" is thus connected to the coming age. In my opinion, this is what led Martin Luther to speak about the two kingdoms – the one that has arrived and the one that will arrive expediently. Dennis Duling summarizes Luther's concept of the two kingdoms:

> Luther sought to purify the church and at the same time to lay foundations for, and set limits to, the state. He often stressed that the individual Christian was ultimately a citizen not of the secular kingdom, but of the spiritual Kingdom of God; yet just as often, he suggested that the Christian individual lives in both the secular kingdom (subject to the secular law and obligated to protect one's neighbor with the instruments of the secular state) and the Kingdom of God (subject to the demands of the Sermon on the Mount). Though the church was not totally severed from the Kingdom, neither was the state, for the Christian was responsible to both.[43]

I conclude that the Kingdom is fulfilled through the liberation of the oppressed, the feeding of the hungry, and the loving of the unloved – and of sinners accepting Jesus as Savior, Lord, and Kingdom.

Salvation or Social Action?

The question of which – salvation or social action – takes priority has been raised and analyzed by different groups. Evangelicals, however, give more attention to this question than any other group.

In *One-Sided Christianity?*, Sider handles this issue thoughtfully and with care. For the author, the two components of the kingdom, evangelism and social action, must be held together – each with its own distinctive characteristics but inseparably bound together. He indicates several points that clarify his position, summarized as follows: [44]

- It is confusing to talk about the repentance and conversion of the nations and its denominational corporations. Corporate structure

---

42. Goldsworthy, "Kingdom of God," 619.
43. Duling, "Kingdom of God," 118.
44. Sider, *One-Sided Christianity?*, 160–165.

can change their policies, but they cannot accept Jesus Christ as personal Lord and Savior, undergo baptism, or become an active member of a local church. Only individual persons can do that.
- Evangelism and social action are distinct because they have different outcomes. Social action may lead to cleaner water, more democracy, or greater economic justice – but having these valuable qualities is simply not the same thing as knowing your sins are forgiven, rejoicing in a personal relationship with Jesus Christ, or knowing you are on the way to living forever in the presence of the risen Lord.
- The intention of evangelism and social action are also distinct. In evangelism, the central intention is to lead non-Christians to becoming disciples of Jesus Christ; social action possesses a central intention of improving the socio-economic or psychological well-being for people during their life here on earth.
- We should distinguish between evangelism and social action in order to protect the integrity of social action. Social action does not need to be conducted as a means of "priming" a community for evangelism, nor should it be done with an evangelistic purpose in mind in order to legitimize it. Social action has its own biblical justification.
- Equating evangelism and social action endangers the integrity of the gospel and the practice of evangelism – and usually, though not inevitably, evangelism gets lost or abandoned over the course of engagement with social action.
- Evangelism and social action are distinct, because the latter can be done without verbal proclamation and outward profession of faith.

Sider concludes from this analysis that, while there is a distinct similarity between the matters of social action and evangelism, they are not the same thing.[45] While evangelism is not identical with social action, Christians are biblically called to do both. Which, then, is the most important?

Sider argues that evangelism must be the priority over social action, and returns to a points-based system to explain his position that can be summarized as follows:[46]

---

45. Sider, 165.
46. Sider, 170–180.

- Evangelism is essential, as it is the means by which to bring new Christians to God. Those Christians will then be responsible for Christian social action.
- There is nothing more important than eternal life, the factor that lies at the heart of Christianity.
- Specialization of action is a legitimate and useful practice, but this does not mean that any Christian should suppose that he or she should solely work toward either evangelism or social action. Every Christian is called to actively engage in both callings.
- The gospel must be presented first – before conducting social action. However, in cases of immediate national, local, or personal emergency – including matters such as endemic starvation or rife hardship – earthly needs must be attended to first.
- Jesus addressed this problem himself, when a scribe asked which was the greatest commandment. Christ replied that there were two greatest commandments: the first was to love God with all one's heart, soul, and mind, while the second was to love one's neighbor as oneself.

It is clear from this that Sider views the evangelism and social action of Jesus as highly significant and enlightening in regard to the primacy of either evangelism or social action. The author sees the importance of both but holds a primary focus on evangelism. He concludes that, while the callings of evangelism and social action are not identical, they are still inseparable.

Sider also points out five specific areas of interrelationship and deep connection between evangelism and social action:[47]

1. The theological framework of biblical evangelism shows that evangelism is inseparable from social action. Christians must give equal attention to repentance of both personal and social sin.

2. Evangelism promotes social action and, because of this, the gospel creates new persons whose transformed lives and characters can change the world.

3. The common life of the church must shape society. When the church truly models what it preaches – when it genuinely breaks through the sinful barriers of racism, class prejudice, and oppression – its very existence has a powerful influence on the larger society.

---

47. Sider, 180–183.

4. Social action has an evangelistic dimension. When we care for people in Jesus's name, our acts of mercy open hearts to the gospel. When we stand with the poor to challenge the way they are treated, they are more likely to accept our invitation to turn to Christ.
5. Social action can help protect the fruits of evangelism by creating an environment in which new believers can be faithful and effective disciples of Jesus.

Sider concludes by stating the following:

> Evangelism and social action are inseparably interrelated. Each one leads to the other. They mutually support each other. In practice, they are often so intertwined that it would be silly and fruitless, indeed destructive, to pull them apart. Evangelism and social action are distinct, approximately equally deserving of resources, and inseparably interrelated.[48]

These are Sider's conclusions about evangelism and social action. It is clear to me that Sider, as an evangelical theologian and social activist, will endeavor, by his views, to assist the church generally – and the evangelical church in particular – to adapt this holistic approach in which evangelism and social action are distinct but inseparable.

Moving on in our assessment, we shift from Sider to the theologian Christopher Wright. Wright argues that the mission of the church is, indeed, the mission of Christ. He believes that the following goals are essential to this mission:[49]

- To proclaim the good news of the kingdom.
- To teach, baptize and nurture new believers.
- To respond to human need by loving service.
- To seek to transform unjust structures of society.
- To strive to safeguard the integrity of creation and to sustain the life of the earth.

From these points, we can surmise that Wright views the mission of the church as evangelism, teaching, compassion, justice, and care of creation:[50]

---

48. Sider, 183.
49. Wright, *Integral Mission*, 3.
50. Wright, 4.

- In evangelism, we proclaim the good news that Jesus Christ is Lord, King, and Savior.
- In teaching, we bring people into maturity of faith and discipleship, in submission to Christ as Lord.
- In compassion, we follow the example of the Lord Jesus, who "went around doing good" (Acts 10:38).
- In seeking justice, we remember that the Lord Jesus Christ is the judge of all earth.
- In using and caring for creation, we are handing what belongs to the Lord Jesus Christ by right of creation and redemption.

Wright argues that these five models of mission can be summarized as follows:[51]

- Building the church through evangelism and teaching, bringing people to repentance, faith, and obedience as disciples of Jesus Christ.
- Serving society through compassion and justice, in response to Jesus sending us into the world to love and serve, to be salt and light, to do good works, and to "seek the peace and prosperity" of the people around us – as Jeremiah told the Israelites in Babylon (Jer 29:7).
- Caring for creation through godly use of the resources of creation, along with ecological concern and action; in doing so, Christians fulfill the very first "great commission" given to humanity in Genesis 1 and 2.

Wright argues that, sometimes, the concept of "holistic mission" is a term used to mean all essential Christians acts except evangelism. Per Wright, "holistic mission" is a kind of bag in which to toss other ministries: social action, medical mission, poverty relief, community development, environmental action, human rights advocacy, working for peace and reconciliation, and so on. Wright disagrees with this approach, and rightly indicates that "holistic mission" – engaging with all addressed ills – must contain all of his named elements. Thus, social action without evangelism is just as non-holistic as is evangelism without social engagement. Holistic mission must include evangelism and not just refer to "everything else."

Wright pushes his argument further, stating that "holistic mission" is sometimes used to mean everything and anything that can be called "mission" – including evangelism – but without integration into corporate values. Holistic

---

51. Wright, 5.

mission becomes a bag of multi-colored marbles, in which evangelism is merely one shiny distraction among any number of shiny distractions which a church may or may not emphasize, or in which an individual might be interested. Mission becomes a smorgasbord of activities, and evangelism is considered just one option among many available ones. Per Wright, this condition is misleading and not in accordance with biblical principles.[52]

In this context, Wright argues that many evangelicals have traditionally spoken of the primacy of evangelism. They do so because, they argue, evangelism addresses the greatest human need. Neither I nor Wright deny this claim, but this framing of the issue keeps the human focus upon those matters of a particularly earthly nature.[53]

Wright concludes:

> So when I speak of the centrality of the gospel and evangelism, I do not mean a center that makes everything else peripheral – marginal and unimportant, "out there, far off from the center." Rather I mean central in the way that a hub is central to a wheel. A wheel is an integrated functioning object, with a rim or tire connected to the road. But the full orb of the rim must be connected at every point to the hub through the spokes. In that sense the hub is the integrating center of all that the wheel is and does. And the hub is connected to the engine, transmitting its power to "where the rubber hits the road." There is no point asking "which is more important – the hub or the rim?" If you haven't got both integrated together, you haven't got a wheel at all. Both are essential and must function together.[54]

One can argue that Christopher Wright sees the integrated model of the whole mission of the church as going beyond priority to integration: a central spoke in the great wheel of mission, connecting all other aspects to each other and to the lordship of Jesus Christ. The Great Commission, however, begins by telling us that Jesus is Lord of all of life within his creation. Jesus is Lord of workplace and the family, Lord of the streets and the skies, Lord of schools and slums, Lord of hospitals and housing, Lord of governments, business, academia, sport, and culture – Lord of all time and space. Thus, the discipleship and mission that Jesus calls us into is meant for every part of every life. If Jesus

---

52. Wright, 7.
53. Wright, 7.
54. Wright, 8.

is Lord of heaven and earth, there is no part of life at all – no job, no vacation, no day or night – that is exempt from the rest of what he says in the Great Commission and all that it refers back to in the rest of the gospel.

Mission is not an agenda to be tackled by people assigned to "do it for the rest of us": rather, mission is the essential mode of existence for the whole life of every member of the Christian church in its entirety. It is clear that both Sider and Wright believe in the holistic model, but it is important to indicate that Wright is preoccupied with evangelism. Per Wright, evangelism should not be lost to social action – rather, the focus of religiously minded efforts should always be oriented toward evangelism.

One could argue that Sider's views can be very helpful in assisting one to understand the nature and purpose of the kingdom of God. The kingdom is a present reality where both evangelism and social action can function together in order to bring about the end of this age and usher in an age-to-come. At this inevitable point, Jesus will return to the earth and consummate his kingdom.

It is clear that Western culture and theology have been influenced by the spiritual theory of humanity's separation into the separate entities of spirit and physical form. I agree with the New Zealand theologian and social activist Viv Grigg, who claims that Jesus – as an ancient Jew – would not have recognized the human dualism that was popularized by the school of Greek philosophy, rather than the predominant rabbinical thought that is confirmed to have influenced him as a Jew. Grigg writes, "Do we work for transformation of the individual or the transformation of the structures of society? These questions come from the Greek separation of man into spirit and body. The Hebrew people, who shared Jesus's concept of life, knew no such dichotomy."[55]

For Grigg, it is clear that there is no such choice between evangelism and social action, no choice between salvation and structural change. He declares: "We are called to save souls. We are called to save the bodies of the children who get sick through the disease of a garbage dump. There is no choice."[56]

The debate between the primacy of either social justice or evangelism is an invalid argument. Grigg is correct in that we have no choice between salvation and social action because a human's body and soul are not separate. In Jesus's teachings, we may sense a focus on evangelism over social action. Outwardly, Jesus's response to the scribe – the importance of the divine commands to love God and to love one's neighbor – seems to support this suggestion. However, if we look at some of Jesus's other words, the subject becomes clearer. Christ

---

55. Grigg, *Companion to the Poor*, 92.
56. Grigg, 93.

stated: "If you are offering your gift at the altar, and there remember that your brother or sister has something against you, leave your gift . . ." (Matt 5:23–34). In this passage, we find that Jesus declares that we cannot build a righteous relationship with God if we have not a righteous relationship with our brothers and sisters. They are conjoined efforts, and both are required by God. In his comments about these verses, the theologian Robert C. Campbell extols, "Even if I am worshiping Almighty God and remember that someone has something against me, I should withhold my worship temporarily until the relationship is established. Nothing is more important than the relationship with another."[57]

From our discussion that the kingdom is a present reality and also a future event, we can confirm that there is no primacy of evangelism or social action. The central problem of a present-focused eschatological interpretation of the kingdom is that it reduces the kingdom – a divine and impossible-to-define concept – to social action. Conversely, the issue of the futuristic eschatological interpretation of the kingdom is that it reduces the heavenly state to evangelism as the only prerequisite to eternal life. Thus, we affirm the following:

- The kingdom is present and future.
- Evangelism and social action are distinct callings.
- Social action has a biblical justification.
- In some cases, evangelism and social action are interrelated.
- There is no primacy of evangelism over social action or social action over evangelism.

The Theology of Samuel Habib

Rev. Dr. Samuel Habib was the founder and general director of the Coptic Evangelical Organization for Social Services (CEOSS) as well as the president of the Protestant Church in Egypt. Additionally, he wrote over forty books, translated a number of others, and generated a theology so rich that it would be effectively impossible to present here in its complete form. I will, however, attempt to present Habib's theology, with an emphasis on its social aspects. Developed in the Egyptian context, this theology calls for social change on a local level.[58]

---

57. Campbell, *Jesus*, 146.

58. The information contained within this section is based upon two important sources: my own experience working alongside Dr. Samuel Habib for eleven years and pages 110–118 of Virtue's poignant text, *Vision of Hope*.

Habib grew up believing that the main task of a church leader was to preach the gospel. He believed that the main focus of a leader trained in theology should be entry into pastoral work; he also saw the value of literature and literacy work, and would eventually go on to devote the years of his young adulthood to providing literacy-based educational services. Habib eventually shifted his focus to serving the poor and illiterates, moving away from pulpit-based preaching as a primary role and calling.

After refocusing his efforts in 1950, the following ten years of Habib's ministry proved to be quite difficult. During the late 1950s, some of the top Christian leaders in Egypt acknowledged the importance of Habib's work and began to promote it as a vital part of the church's ministry. While his efforts became more focused on social ministry, Habib began to assess the biblical justifications of this shift in mission.

As Habib read the Bible, particularly the Gospels, he developed a deeper understanding of Jesus's mission. In the parable of the Ten Lepers, he saw an effort parallel to his own: Jesus cured ten lepers, and only one returned at a later time to thank him for his blessing. The other nine lepers were never present in the gospel text but, despite this, their well-being was still important to Christ. The efforts he undertook to cure their bodies speaks to the importance he placed on them as human beings – a value in itself, apart from whether they accepted him as Lord and Savior or not. The one who returned and thanked him was given a second chance to know Jesus and believe him in a deeper way. After he was cured, this man established a belief in the holy qualities of Jesus.

From this parable, Habib surmised that Christ had two central missions. The first was the mission of evangelism, primarily focused upon the mission of helping people learn and know of Jesus Christ as Lord and Savior. The second goal was to assist people with becoming *more fully human* – human beings as God had created them at the beginning of history. Jesus wanted people to be cured of their ills, and to find happiness; thus, Habib opposed the belief that it was by God's will that his fellow Egyptians should live in pain or poverty.

Habib spoke on the subject in the following way:

> If we look at the doctrine of creation, God created all people equal. Because of sin, situations of social injustice emerged: feudal lords and masters became the oppressor, and servants and slaves became the oppressed. Women became enslaved to men and injustices mounted down through the ages. Our role as Christians is to copy Jesus' ministry, and to help communities regain their history as

recorded in Genesis 1 and 2 – the Creation, as God intended it before sin entered in Genesis 3.[59]

In this way, Habib asserts, Jesus wanted God's will in creation to be implemented: "Men and women would be equal, as would masters and slaves, rich and poor. The dignity of all human beings would be respected, asserted, and supported."[60]

Habib maintained that as we look at the New Testament, we can see situations where Jesus healed people without ever preaching to them. We also see situations in which Jesus preached to people without healing them. There are also situations in which Jesus both healed people and preached to the masses at the same time. From these instances, Habib concluded that it is possible that Jesus's healing ministry can be seen as an end in itself, while the ministry of reconciliation – that is, of bringing people to a saving faith in Jesus Christ – is a separate goal. Both goals are a responsibility of the church and coexist along parallel lines, each complementing the other.

Jesus respected the dignity of all human beings. Habib observed that thousands of people who were healed by Jesus Christ were never saved in his lifetime. Some of them heard the gospel and accepted it, and others did not hear the gospel at all. Despite these differences, Jesus nonetheless hoped that they would be healed simply because they were human beings.

The doctrines of creation and atonement are the two most important beliefs in the Bible. They complement one another and cannot be separated from one another. Over the course of time, the church of Jesus Christ became so fully involved with the doctrine of atonement that it neglected the doctrine of creation.

The doctrine of creation shows us that God is the Father of all humanity no matter their race, color, gender, or religion. The whole world is his world. In this way, if Jesus were here today in Egypt, he would serve both Muslims and Christians. He would not separate or distinguish between peoples. We have only to look at the manner in which Christ dealt with both the Jew and the Samaritan: the two clearly differed in their doctrines, but Jesus did not favor the Samaritan over the Jew or vice versa. Instead, he viewed them both as sons and daughters of creation.

Our misunderstanding comes from not seeing our role as dual in nature. We must see both the humanity of men and women as intrinsic in itself, while also viewing humanity's need for salvation through Christ as another separate, but equal, necessity. Habib saw this virtue embodied in Jesus's support

---

59. Virtue, *Vision of Hope*, 93.
60. Virtue, 93.

of women: what Jesus did for the Samaritan woman, for instance, was not respected by his Jewish community. His respect for the woman who had engaged in adultery, and his support for women in general, showed that he demonstrated an intrinsic equality between all men and women.

In his commentary regarding the matter of divine equality, Habib cited the instance of the adulterous woman and the willingness of the Jewish leaders to stone her to death. By his decision to deny an opportunity to condemn her in favor of forgiving her, Jesus intended to display that the man involved in the incident was also complicit in sin. Both are equally guilty before God: both need to repent, like the self-righteous Jewish community. Habib saw in Jesus's support of both women and men, children and outcasts, the human dignity of all people without exception.

In the story of the blind Bartimaeus, Habib saw the issue of restoring dignity as more important than the restoring of physical sight. This is a common occurrence along the path of Christ's ministry, as seen in his consistent support of low-caste people: the poor, women, and children. The church should be involved in this ministry of Jesus as if the church were Jesus himself.

Habib believed that Christ's actions had political implications for the community at large. In reference to Jesus's entrance into Jerusalem, Habib noted the celebratory parade prepared by his followers; in contrast, Jesus chose to ride a donkey into the city – a humble and common means for the Son of God to arrive in his city on Passover. The crowds shouted to him and recognized his leadership, but Jesus did not wish to be a leader in a sense understood by his followers. He saw his leadership as a way to change society into one that understood God, believed in God, and was guided by God-given ethics.

Habib argued that Jesus saw no separation between faith, the church, and religion. The leaders of the community were also the leaders in the synagogue; the two roles were explicitly intertwined. Habib interpreted Jesus's attempt to purify the temple as a very serious attack on the power of the day's top political and religious leaders. As these men were the most prominent property owners and money lenders, Jesus attacked the merchants of the temple; in his effort to achieve social change, Christ's outburst was directed at the leadership of the Jewish people and against their temple. He desired a society built upon the ethics of faith, rather than a society built upon sin.

If we look at what Jesus Christ did, we see him wanting to help the community – and the society at large – to step back and assess its ethical framework. He hoped to help others consider ethical issues seriously: to do justice, to be honest, and to be loyal to the general cause of humanity rather than ambitiously seek earthly power or status.

When we look critically at our brothers and sisters, we cannot separate the spiritual matters of people from the social or economic realities of their lives. They are all one, linked in a complex and detailed manner:

> If I am honest, I am honest when I pray and in my commerce. I am honest in my relationships with my friends. We must see human beings in their wholeness. We must not categorize people into different parts, i.e. the spiritual, the social, or the material. All are one, and all must be viewed as one.[61]

All human beings have a common humanity and unity – and if we intend to take care of people, we must treat the whole person. By focusing only on an individual's spiritual life, we forget that this individual also consists of flesh and blood. A hungry person will never hear the message, because they are swamped by poverty and hunger; thus, we must take care of those problems before we attempt to minister to a person's spiritual needs. These matters will be more deeply explored in the fifth chapter of this work.

The church, from the beginning, has been concerned for the poor. It has given money and food for the hungry on certain occasions. Helping people in this way is good, but it is not enough. Relief is only a part of the picture. A person can become dependent on those who give them help; this is ultimately not good. We need to be involved in development. In development, we help the person find a craft that gives them regular work. One major problem with aid is that it puts one person over another. It puts the receiver in the position of the supplicant and does not recognize the equality of all human beings. Whereas, if we work together, and the poor person is given a loan and repays it over a period of time, we stand on equal footing. That person is not dependent on me, but independent of me. They are a respected person in their own right.

It is time that the church brings together the theological and biblical issues with the social and developmental issues, so that individuals – or groups of individuals, or communities – become more empowered to discover resources for their own development, so they can achieve better lives. This has been one of the most neglected areas in the church's life down through the years, and it must be reclaimed. It means the development of new institutional specializations, bolstered by study and technical assistance. It is a task that the church must take seriously and be responsible for, along with preaching the gospel of Jesus Christ to lost sinners.

---

61. Virtue, 94.

Models for Christian Engagement

It is wonderful to believe in the truth, especially if one reaches this truth through one's own study and investigation. The life of Jesus is crucial, and his message is important for any Christian approach to the ministry. As a result of the study done for this book, I have become more convinced that the biblical records we have today contain historical data about the life of Jesus and his ministry. The early church shaped this information to better assist the first Christian communities with comprehending Christ's message and evangelism. The authentic voice of Jesus in the gospels' final form is very clear.

In summary, there are three main interpretations of the nature of the kingdom:

1. The first interpretation is based on the concept of the kingdom as a present reality. This approach focused on social action as the main means by which the Christian community will bring about the kingdom.

2. The second interpretation is based on the concept of the kingdom as a future event. This approach focuses on evangelism as the main means by which to bring people to eternal life: to save souls is the only absolute way of bringing people into the future kingdom.

3. The third interpretation is based on the concept of the kingdom as both a present reality and a future event. In this approach, evangelism and social action are equally important. This approach can be further sub-divided into three main perspectives:
   a) Social action is a prerequisite effort for successful evangelism; the ultimate goal is saving souls.
   b) Social action and evangelism are equal in importance and could be separate efforts. This idea comes from the concept that Jesus had two different ministries: one for evangelism and one for social action.
   c) The holistic perspective, which believes that evangelism and social action are inseparable, interrelated, and must be enacted together. One leads to the other, and both missions equally support each other.

When we look critically at these approaches, we can see that the methodology behind interpretation 3b – proposed by Samuel Habib – could be viewed as quite progressive by the standards of Egyptian society and the evangelical church. Interpretation 3c (as proposed by Sider and Wright) could be an appropriate fit for the church in Egypt but may not be a functional approach for working within the greater Egyptian culture.

The church needs a theology by which it can develop different approaches to fit the many needs of the society in which it exists. There is no single model to fit every situation. Therefore, the church must decide which direction it will take and develop a model appropriate for that direction. A model based on interpretation 3b may be an appropriate alternative for use by faith-based organizations and religious institutions in enacting community change when the focus is a matter of social responsibility – that is, an effort independent of mission. A model based on interpretation 3c, on the other hand, might be most appropriate for efforts in which evangelism and social action go hand-in-hand. The primacy of either could be determined by cultural and infrastructural needs over time, allowing this interpretation to remain flexible in changing times. If the church could engage in both efforts simultaneously, its holistic mission would be fulfilled readily; if the situation becomes more difficult or tenuous, however, an evolving approach may be the most beneficial one.

It is very important to distinguish the different aspects of the Christian mission. Holistic Christian mission can be summarized in Paul's words to his disciple, Timothy: "So that the servant of God may be thoroughly equipped for every good work" (2 Tim 3:17). The salvation of Christ aims for a complete person – that is, renewed on spiritual, psychological, physical, and social levels.

The completeness of humanity is the final, essential target of salvation and Christian mission. This effort can be accomplished via work in two basic fields: the spiritual field, and the social field.

The very basis of humanity's spiritual renewal is the restoration of humanity's relationship with God. This ethic is the core proclamation of Christianity and the foundation of the Christian life. If Christians can proclaim this message of restoration, then they have declared the whole gospel of salvation clearly and straightforwardly. This aspect of salvation focuses on the individual relationship between God and humanity, and less on humanity's interactions with one another.

There is another face of salvation, however: the social aspect. If we are willing to assess the significance of the communal qualities of spiritually renewing salvation, then we will be better able to comprehend the broader concept of salvation. Though an integral part of salvation, it is not just an individual's relationship with God that determines the state of their faith: rather, salvation is communal and preoccupied with the social renewal of society.

Much of our understanding of Christianity focuses upon the arrival of the kingdom of God – that once-and-future apocalyptic event, intervening in our history – as a popularly accepted prerequisite for achieving humanity's completeness. We believe that this restored future reality – one longed for by humanity – has already arrived in the mission of Jesus Christ. People living in his time expected the ready intervention of God to rule over the earth and establish his kingdom during their lifetimes: an imminent and cataclysmic manifestation of God's full mission. The kingdom of God represents the hopes of the people who lived in the time of Jesus, representing the restoration of social justice and a true recovery of human dignity.

It is of utmost importance to understand that either facet of this mission – the first being one's personal relationship with God, the second being communal in nature – is wholly complete, in and of itself. Proclaiming the gospel out loud and embodying the gospel practically are both equivalent methods of communicating the "good news." These different methods are both legitimate when conducted in an honest and forthright manner with those people who live alongside us in society. Thus, the gospel we should advocate is *the whole gospel for the whole person.*

The relationship between the proclaimed message of the gospel and the executed practice of the gospel is a nuanced one and requires some exploration. As Samuel Habib developed his understanding of Jesus's mission, he believed that it was a two-fold effort: in his life, Christ showed that social action and the gospel message should go hand-in-hand.

It is significant to note that, as part of his mission, Jesus conducted a number of his ministries without offering the recipients a verbal proclamation of the gospel, or even expecting that they would see the spiritual significance of his assistance. In assessing the account of Christ and the Canaanite woman (Matt 15:22–28), we only note that she requests assistance – not salvation – from Jesus (v. 25). Moreover, Jesus offered her the healing of her daughter without an attempt at traditional evangelism. This miracle story, as Matthew depict it narratively, shows the readiness of Jesus's response to the needs of a destitute woman – one who was not a Christian, and one who may never have become one. It reveals Jesus's compassion toward those experiencing poverty, especially when those people are members of marginalized social groups, such as women and girls.

In a different account, we see Jesus heal the servant of the Roman centurion – a respected and overtly powerful political figure in contemporary society (Luke 7:1–10). Again, we note that the centurion asked only that Jesus heal his servant: Jesus did not preach to him, nor did he verbally proclaim the gospel to him. Nevertheless, Jesus responded to his request by living out the gospel in a practical way by healing his servant's maladies. As shown in Luke's narrative, a striking aspect of this account is how Jesus readily interacted with the political authorities of his day. Jesus made an effort to utilize his resources to assist this political leader, duly aware that fulfilling his social mission was of great importance.

There are many accounts in the life of Christ that show how the embodied practice of the gospel was, in and of itself, a holistic presentation of the good news. Consequently, missional communication of the gospel as the message of salvation did not prevent a lively embodiment of the quest of God to bring humanity to its complete and whole form in Jesus's ministry.

In essence, the social responsibility of the church is actually an application of its doctrine of incarnation. Jesus himself was an embodiment of God bestowed upon humanity in order to be able to bring humanity into fellowship with God and one other. In order to save humanity, God incarnated in space and time as a man; in the same manner, preaching the gospel represents the same spiritual trajectory. The social responsibility of the church is another of the methods utilized by Christ to spread the "good news." In other words, just as God incarnated and lived among humans to restore qualitative life to them, his church has a social responsibility – a follow-up to Christ's incarnation – to aid humanity in moving toward God.

Essential to the spiritual and ethical growth of our faith is the "bridging of the gap" between Jesus and the church. It is important to note that if the church, in the context of existing within a pluralistic society containing practitioners of different religions, develops a transparent social mission in an effort to achieve the kingdom of God – accompanied by no hidden agenda of evangelism, in a manner akin to Christ's ministry – then that church can truly embody its mission. Through such efforts, a church may engage fully with civil society and become an agent of change through the development and institution of programs focused around the promotion of social responsibility.

To reiterate, today's church has three models for its mission (based in an understanding of the kingdom as both a present reality and a future event):

1. Within the first model (based on interpretation 3a), the church can proclaim the message of the gospel through the preaching of salvation, as well as the history and theological content of the "good news."

2. Within the second model (based on interpretation 3b), the church can proclaim its message of the gospel through the embodiment of this message in a practical and communal manner.

3. Within the third model (based on interpretation 3c) – the integral and holistic model – the church can proclaim its verbal and preached message of the gospel while also embodying the gospel via contextual social engagement.

Essential to all three of these models is a "theology of transparency" – a spiritual standard that forbids us to conduct our social mission as an application of a hidden agenda or as a subtle form of evangelism. To the contrary, it must be shown that the church is conducting its mission to aid the God-given society in which it exists – as, after all, human beings were created in the image of the divine. This does not mean that the church is to disregard its mission of proclamation via evangelism, but that alternate venues must also be considered. Our emphasis here is on the utmost importance of the clarity and transparency of the church's social mission as an effort conducted for the sake of the health and wellness of society, and not as a means by which one could "fish" for congregants.

If the church engages in this transparent holistic mission and regards the social mission as a complete mission in and by itself, engagement with civil society is an effective and transparent alternative to verbal evangelism. In this context, faith-based organizations were born as a means by which to live out the idea that the social mission is a mission of itself. Thus, the church can directly engage in socially responsible mission or create sub-organizations to achieve this goal.

Since its establishment, the Presbyterian Church of Egypt has been careful to offer social services to many multi-religious communities spread throughout the country, provided hand-in-hand alongside its spiritual services. Thus, as the church building and sanctuary were built, the hospitals and schools were built at the same time. The Presbyterian Church of Egypt prioritized building schools for boys and girls, especially in poor neighborhoods. As early as 1927, the number of these schools reached seventy-eight. Additionally, the church responded to health problems in different areas in Egypt by founding various hospitals and health-care service centers. By the second half of the nineteenth century, the church had constructed a number of hospitals in Assuit, Tanta, and Cairo.

In conclusion, the social responsibility of the church and the verbal proclamation of the gospel are not two opposing and different options. They are both equivalent responsibilities and should be undertaken through creative venues – through an integrative and honest methodology based on transparent theology. The embodied practice of the good news is no less important than the verbal proclamation of it!

The church has faced difficulty in recognizing the marginalized members of society. These populations live in poor conditions and are oppressed by society itself: they face consistent difficulties in overcoming social barriers, making it impossible for them to assume a proper and dignified position in society. The church has tended to write them off as "lazy," and therefore unable to truly change the nature of their situation. As a socially oriented institution, the church has a responsibility to assist these people and thus must recognize this responsibility as derived through the teachings of Jesus.

The church's position in regard to women must be defined more clearly. The kingdom does not discriminate between men and women, but the church has done so and continues to do so. The New Testament texts consistently demonstrate the equality of the sexes. This understanding carries with it a social imperative – and the church, in its ministry, has a responsibility to work toward this equality.

In conclusion, it became clear throughout this chapter that Jesus challenges the church to fight against darkness. The Sermon on the Mount calls people to repent and to move closer to God. Jesus's very mission was wholly holistic. His concept of the kingdom was present as he worked hard to change the situations of those living around him. His concept of the kingdom was futuristic and progressive, as he was always looking to the age to come. I hope that the church rereads the gospel, understands the concept of the kingdom in its original context in the Gospels, and develops a model that represents the gospel as the truly dynamic word of God.

3

The Church and Coexistence

The concept of "coexistence" refers to the process by which a person or group learns to live alongside people practicing a different way of life than their own; the goals of coexistence include acceptance of diversity, an ability to engage effectively with the diverse individual(s), and the maintenance of a positive relationship with this "other" person or group of people. In 1956, Nikita Khrushchev (1894–1971), acting as the first secretary of the Soviet Union, put into effect "peaceful coexistence," a foreign policy that attempted to contrast the hostility of the West with the diplomatic nature of those nations within the Soviet bloc.[1] In developing his theory, Khrushchev seems to have displayed his appreciation of the doctrine of coexistence, which emerged from the horrors of World War II. After its new implementation as part of the Cold War, the concept of coexistence was applied to sectarian conflict: thus, a modified variant of the same theory put forth by Khrushchev was applied to ongoing inter-religious conflicts and conflict in societies divided by affiliation (by sect, religion, doctrine, language, or physiology).

Within this new framework, coexistence focuses upon one society's relationship with "the other": an anomalous moniker, applied to any individual or group that exists outside of the society's mainstream preferences. "The other" exists, and this existence requires society make an effort to understand "the other" to the best of its ability. The eventual goal of a society employing this ideal is true coexistence: different societal groups living side-by-side, comprehending and respecting one another in the social, ideological, linguistic, and national/regional arenas regardless of differences related to race, creed, gender, or social status.

---

1. ʿAbd El-Fattaḥ, "Oṭor Mo'assasyya."

Therefore, coexistence is not limited to the post-World War II world, the Cold War, or the field of ideological conflict. If applied to societal matters, the coexistence framework promotes constructive discussion among disparate groups: for example, opposing economic classes or cultural entities that possess differing opinions regarding social matters (such as the acceptance of women in popular society) are led to constructive dialogue when they acknowledge the necessity of coexistence. One could apply this framework of coexistence to modern citizenship: without it, shared life within a diverse society – political, social, or economic – lacks a solid foundation on which to survive.

Church, Citizenship, and Coexistence

If applied non-intersectionally, the political concept of citizenship – bereft of social, economic, and cultural considerations – is not a useful tool in the building of a pluralistic and equal society. Citizenship is a broad concept that must consider the aforementioned factors and consider elements of life well beyond state membership and political participation. The concept and reality of citizenship goes well beyond theoretical political equality between separate classes and groups of people: an honest practice of citizenship is linked to active justice work and societal transformation, and should, thus, not be limited to "justice" as defined by any one overly regulative, socially restrictive legal system. While legal support of justice efforts is welcome, I believe that justice must be implemented in a more holistic manner. It is my view that sustainable justice efforts – sincere attempts to bring the culturally divergent members of a society together on equal participatory footing, be it in the common markets or the stately halls of power – are possible only when the church recognizes and adapts to its contextual political and cultural realities.[2]

Keeping these points in mind, I posit that the works of the church – namely, its essential social efforts and adaptive implementations of theology – be directed toward the society in which it exists. There is an ongoing dialectical relationship between the theological mission of the church and the popular role of that same institution. When the church readily interacts with the community in order to build awareness and encourage common participation in its visions of change, these changes often manifest; interacting with society as it evolves, too, is an important act in which the church must engage. The church has great capacity to support society as it shifts toward progressive development and aims toward social enlightenment; on the other hand, avoiding taking part

---

2. Zaki, "Al Taʿayoush," 57.

in community dialogue may have detrimental effects upon the culture or the church, including failure to realize and implement transformative change in either or both entities.

Accordingly, the church must acknowledge the necessity of, and develop a theology of, concern for public affairs – and not just as a means to an end, but also as a true and faithful theological orientation. Certainly, the church believes in the necessity of accepting Christ as one's personal savior; following up on this belief by righteously engaging in public affairs – and doing so in a manner that works to satisfy humanity's natural, physical, and moral needs – acts only as confirmation of this belief. As a Christian, belief in Christ as savior acts as a point of guidance, and even an endorsement, for public participation: both are key and complementary parts in his great mission of salvation for humankind and are essential precedents for the proclamation of the kingdom of God in this world.

As we see in this new era of Christian pluralism and acceptance of "the other," coexistence stands as one of the most important and foundation aspects of socially effective and Christ-led theology. Old Testament figures often spoke of the stark distinction of Israel as God's chosen people, and regularly associated religion with matters such as nationalism and genealogy; although his primary focus was on the Jewish community, Jesus promoted a universal and cross-cultural message that readily superseded cultural exceptionalism – doing so while preaching to and healing the citizens of other nations. The apostle Paul worked to support Christ's gospel of coexistence: he asserted that not all nations needed to convert to Judaism before Christianity, an indication of the boundary-transcending and stereotype-averse nature of this faith.

Today, the church must live the message as put forth by Christ. Despite our current ecclesiastical reality, it is essential that our institution develop new means by which to engage in public affairs. Regardless of the many contradictory trends that lend to religious polarization in the world, we need – more than ever – a theology of participation. It is the thought of the marginalized and the vulnerable that drives the church to participate in the eternal struggle to free human beings from sin, fear, injustice, hunger, and oppression. The church strives to complete Christ's message of spreading justice, peace, and love in this world. It is to the world's benefit that the church play the role of the once-maligned "Good Samaritan": not knowing the identity or character of a wounded person on the road, the church nevertheless heals their wounds, soothes their pain, and renews their life.[3]

---

3. Zaki, *Al-Aqbat wa Al-Thawrah*, 101.

The Theological Basis for Coexistence

Although considered a contemporary concept, coexistence is a principle deeply rooted in the Holy Bible. For instance, the story of creation in the Old Testament can be interpreted as a model of pluralism: human, animal, plant, and place – while all distinct and fulfilling separate roles – interact fruitfully and prosper because of this interaction. The whole Bible, with both testaments, emphasize diversity; additionally, the divine allowance for men and women from outside the nation of Israel to perform sacred duties supplements this concept further. Additionally, the New Testament displays the good news that can emerge from struggles related to diversity: Paul's steadfast work among the Gentiles and his opposition to the Judaization of nascent Levantine congregations act as important guideposts along the path of coexistence. Existing customs and traditions in Judea act as stumbling blocks for the first Christians; over time, however, the Bible presents diversity as a uniting factor, accepting others' differences as a Christian ideal, and cross-cultural learning a matter of common ground.[4]

The modern world is one of confusion, sadness, and anxiety. In the news, we see war, violence, and disaster across the nations. The gap between the rich and the poor has widened dramatically in recent years because of widespread injustice, corruption, and greed in all social spheres; once-trusted governments, institutions, and individuals engage in these behaviors as a matter of course. As citizens of the Arab world, we are deeply concerned about the atmosphere of tension that has risen throughout the region; conflicts in Palestine, Iraq, Syria, Sudan, Libya, and elsewhere join other ongoing crises, including a harsh and mutual rejection between East and West. These issues act as red flags, indicating the fundamental areas of Arab society that require the church's attention.

Throughout the church's history, schools of thought regarding its position on societal integration have emerged – all with their own views on matters such as social, political, and national responsibility. Several opposing beliefs exist in relation to how the church should best influence the culture in which it exists – morally or socially, politically or economically – as well as whether the church should endeavor to influence culture at all. I believe that both the "theology of creation" and the "theology of redemption" deserve strong and central emphases in the church's social and political consciousness. The divine concept of God as the creator of the world informs the role of the church as his institution: as God created and cared for humankind both spiritually and materially, God's church must act to support this same purpose. God gave

---

4. Zaki, "Al Ta'addodyya," 2184.

humans full individual and social rights; in return, humans are accountable to God in their actions and relationships, as well as for the world left to future generations.[5] The church's most important role is to restore to humans the image and ideal of God stolen from them by slavery and oppression, so they may one day possess the capacity to be fully humane in their treatment of others and in their treatment of themselves.

In proclaiming his good news, Christ did not seek to dissolve all peoples and nations into a singular Christian bloc; rather, his purpose in spreading the gospel was to fill the hearts and minds of those diverse peoples who willingly accepted the message. Those who received this message belonged to a new group, while still maintaining their prior identities. A diversity of races, cultures, and languages populated early – and now, modern – Christian congregations. Heralding the biblical values of equality and respect, this new group calls for the liberation of all creation: for once humanity regains its dignity, freedom, and self-sufficiency, creation will be resplendent and restored once more. In this context, we cannot separate civilization from society: the earthly civilization is subject to its society, which divides one civilization from another – and then divides that one civilization further into groups, peoples, and rival nation states.

As civilization is an earthly concept and not a divine one, we can conclude that there is no one sacred civilization – or, for that matter, one group identity that overrules all others. Attempts at sanctifying civilization have resulted in grave harm to society, human freedoms, and religion: progress and development fall back to better accommodate the newly sanctified state. I believe that it is necessary to distinguish clearly between spiritual/theological values (as linked to religion) and societal values (as linked to civilization); in doing so, we preserve our outlook on the essence and origins of those values, as well as the potential danger of mixing or muddling them.

From these points, we can surmise that the message of the gospel calls for interaction and integration without a loss of subjectivity. Although Christianity originated in the land of the Jewish people, the first churches refused to assimilate into the dominant Jewish culture. Instead, early Christians – including Paul, a formerly Jewish man whose work among non-Jews ensured the cultural and theological diversity of the faith – engaged with non-Jewish civilizations and lent their values to those societies. There is no doubt that integration into those new groups and civilizations was an immense challenge to the sanctified nature of Christianity – I believe, however, that retirement

---

5. Zaki, "Al Masyḥyoun Al-'arab wal Mowaṭana," 2077.

from worldly matters and avoidance of cross-cultural engagement are far greater risks. A group that secludes itself collapses around itself: the journey begins when its members eye "the other" with suspicion and ends with that group's blood and effort being wasted. In reality, integration does not require total agreement on beliefs and ideas; it begins with respect for the beliefs and ideas of "the other" and continues with a refusal to offend or challenge. Protection from assimilation and loss of identity comes through the building and implementation of a culture of diversity, pluralism, and cooperation.

The Holy Bible proclaims that human beings were created for the divine purpose of experiencing dignity, equality, and responsibility. The gospel emphasizes that human equality is in natural accordance with biblical principles – if God created all human beings equally in his image, how can people allow themselves to discriminate against other divinely created human beings? The God-given responsibility of humankind instructs us to love and serve one another; in turn, we must fight for the rights of one another and do so even if it means giving up our personal rights. When a conflict emerged between members of an early church, Paul wrote to them under the leadership of the Holy Spirit. In language that was beautifully metaphoric, the apostle compared the different congregants to the cooperative organs of the human body working toward a common goal. A doctrine of "oneness in diversity, diversity in oneness" can have harmonious results, particularly when all "organs" of a body act according to the directives of the "brain" – or, in this case, God.

Even individually and without community, every human being – gifted as they have been by God, with fruitful and immortal souls – possesses immense worth. According to the Old Testament, one human soul has more value than all of God's other creations. Humans are the caretakers of the earth, the image and example of their creator. Drawing from the New Testament, Christians believe that Christ's arrival on earth to preach the gospel was intended to inspire and invite every person to the kingdom of heaven; in doing so, Christ led humankind to understand their infinite value.[6]

After centuries of massacres, revenge, and rejection of "the other," God calls upon the Christian community to embody the message of Jesus. In one of his speeches, Patriarch Ignatius IV courageously called upon Christians to abide by human rights, serving and respecting all of their fellow peoples.[7] As confirmed in these words by the venerable patriarch, dealing fairly and

---

6. Qolta, *Naḥno wa Al-Akher*, 38.
7. Ashgy, "Al Ḥodor Al-Masiḥi."

graciously with others is an act of faith; consequently, it is fair to conclude that the spiritual mission of the church is inseparable from its social mission. God is not meant to be the only recipient of the love flowing through the human heart; it should also be oriented to one's fellow human beings. The church's march toward the bounties of the heavenly kingdom are thus not distracted by temporal and earthly affairs; on the contrary, its commitment to all that is human only contributes to its righteous orientation and determination. To this end, it is essential that the church do all it can to ease humanity's pain in all its forms and promote the upright development of all peoples.

Modern Christian theology emphasizes the principles of coexistence as essential to religious life. Transcending issues of race, theologians and congregations call for the removal of all cultural restrictions and instead favor genuine interaction and commingling between people. "The other" is no longer impure and forbidden but part of a greater whole. Christ shattered the Old Testament's prohibition on sharing a meal with non-believers, which was later reinforced by the actions of the apostles and other major church figures who reached across the aisle of faith. When confronted with the prospect of conflict, the apostle Peter retreated from engagement with Gentiles, but the apostle Paul rebuked him and stressed the need for Christians to affirm new social values in the same way as Jesus. Cultural mixing and honest dealing with "the other" are the essence of the gospels, and Christ's revolutionary proclamations decrying previous religious and societal restrictions can thus be considered a precedent for the grand project of coexistence.[8]

In contrast to the universality of Christ's message, earthly humanity must still interact with earthly entities that serve to separate one person from another. Systems of government based on nationalism and citizenship, for instance, can act in opposition to an individual's personal relationship with God and his divine call for coexistence. Further, the interaction between religion and politics has led to sharp conflict between national identity on one hand and faith identity on the other. The separation of religious belief from political practice is an evolving matter, changing often because of matters such as geographical boundaries, shifting national affiliations, and progress made toward religious pluralism in different regions. In some cases, religion has had the positive capacity to influence the conscience of a nation, testing or strengthening the political viability of the existing political system. Thus, there are contexts in which religion and politics can work to bolster one another while also enriching the populations served by both institutions.

---

8. Zaki, Al-*Aqbaṭ wa Al-Thawra*, 112.

In the context of Patriarch Ignatius IV's speech, we must consider the matter of political theology: a form of religious discourse that presents a specific vision of faith's manifestation, compete with an associated values system relevant to the public and political lives of its adherents. These values often include integrity and service, solidarity and cooperation, entrepreneurship, and an emphasis on dialogue and aversion to risk. According to the patriarch, the authentic religious adherent will live a political life in line with their faith: they actively participate in society, emphasize the development of social justice and peace, and show respect for the lives of fellow citizens.[9] Directing his words at each person as an individual and not just as part of a greater community, the patriarch promotes intellectual principles and a values system associated with public life – not linked to religious identity, ethnic origin, or any other possible superseding qualifier.

I believe that the religious orientation of Egypt – a place where multiple religious groups participate in public society and prosper as a result – is rooted in ancient history. With appropriate values and public participation, any politician (ancient or modern) would benefit from giving space to religious beliefs: if participatory and contributive, religious belief can bolster the foundations of a safe society for its members. In ancient Egypt, the dominant religion – a set of beliefs and rituals acknowledged since the Predynastic Period and more than three thousand years old – underwent periods of major transformation and development and proved capable of supporting essential values such as pluralism and tolerance. Every Egyptian city had a patron deity, but we have never learned of religious wars, intolerance, or extremism among these adherents of different deities.

The spirit of Egyptian religious tolerance has continued to develop and change over time. Dominant in the beginning of the twentieth century, popular religious pluralism remained in effect until 23 July 1952. It existed in a form of "restricted pluralism" in the eras of Egyptian presidents Gamal A'bdel Nasser and Anwar El-Sadat. The positive steps taken toward political pluralism during the early part of Nasser's era began to topple after the country's military defeat on 5 June 1967. Following Sadat's presidency, the trend of restricted pluralism subsequently continued under President Hosni Mubarak.

After the January 25 Revolution, many Egyptians have begun to speak openly of politics again. A large percentage of the population readily participates in public action and justice efforts, a change I believe to be transformative for society. In my opinion, the launching and strengthening of a political party

---

9. Daw, "Bayna Al-Lahot Al-Syasi."

is less important than the substance of that party: well thought-out political programs, trained political cadres, distinct public relations networks, and appropriate geographical distribution are all factors that act to endorse political and societal participation. Additionally, the issue of religious reform is of distinct prominence as Egypt lacks faith movements oriented around social justice, such as the liberation theology of Latin American. Although addressed during the revolution, the matter of religious reform in politics was left to the unknown. As the public observed the more obvious effects of political change, organizations including the Muslim Brotherhood filled the religious power vacuum.

Within its modern and historical contexts, Egypt faces several distinct challenges to the process of coexistence. Some of these concerns include:

- The popularity of negative/prejudiced beliefs about other religious/sectarian groups, ethnic groups, and regional groups.
- The role of clerical authorities who attempt to divide society on religious lines, reminding Egyptians of their extra-national affiliations/beliefs and attempting to separate one group from another.
- Inaccurate information about other religious groups contained within spiritual and theological texts; these errors become popularized because of the use of these texts in religious educational institutions.
- The effectiveness of state/governmental law when applied to sectarian conflicts, as it can prove to be socially problematic when we apply local legal customs instead of nationally defined law.
- The inherited culture of religious discrimination practiced by some members of society who hold power.

Religion and Power

It is evident that religious extremism became connected to factors such as legal matters, cultural identities, and national commitments. This development proved to have the ability to replace the late twentieth century's prominent political ideologies – especially those pertaining to the politics of identity. It could be argued that the history of most religious traditions is directly related to the history of compromise with the sources of political power; this type of compromise can be observed today in the wide range of relationships between politics and religion, many of which stemmed from efforts to integrate separate ideologies within the same political region.

The story of Joseph in the Old Testament is an accurate display of this kind of relationship. While imprisoned, Joseph developed a reputation as being able to interpret dreams; before long, he was summoned to stand in front of the pharaoh and ordered to divine that lord's subconscious. He became a close confidante of the monarch and was eventually nominated as the prime minister of Egypt. The governmental system subsequently developed by Joseph was used for a millennium afterward. The power of the pharaoh increased, and with it increased Joseph's power, as he rose in prominence and power. The Jewish people joined him in this upward mobility – thus, the status of this group was tied to the power and stability of the state and its affiliated figures.

This arrangement worked out both positively and negatively for the Jewish people. Per tradition, the pharaoh with whom Joseph was employed was the last leader of the Hyksos: an invading western Asiatic nation referred to as *heqa khasut* ("rulers of foreign lands") by the ancient Egyptians. Over time, the Egyptian population grew restive under the rule of the Hyksos; after much effort, an indigenous Egyptian dynasty from Upper Egypt pushed the Hyksos out of the region and replaced them as the lords of Lower Egypt. In accordance with this turn of events, those groups who had been allied to the Hyksos – including Joseph's Jewish people – fell out of influence, along with the governmental system developed by Joseph. The local population had united with the Upper Egyptian regime to topple the Hyksos leadership – and, in doing so, brought down those religiopolitical groups that had become tied to the old hierarchy of power.

As we see from this example, it is important for a religious group to keep its relationship with political power strong in order to survive. This relationship should be characterized by mutual support and consistent engagement with mutual political concerns, despite the waxing and waning of either counterpart's cultural relevance or power. When a religious group becomes intertwined with the power structure of a nation or state, however, the religious group will collapse alongside the nation or state. On the other hand, new and creative approaches to this dichotomy can produce different results: new relationships can be built between institutions of power, groups practicing specific religious traditions, and those representing different segments of society. The creation of a cooperative arrangement between political powers and supportive societal groups can benefit the greater society, including those who chose not to take part in its development. Another aspect of the challenges related to religious traditions is when a culture plays "host" to religious traditions that originated outside of that cultural context.[10]

When we look at the relationship between religion and power from a theological perspective, our doctrine of creation affirms that the one God who created all things – our loving God, who has been intrinsic in all creation from the beginning of time – is, as declared in the Bible, God of all nations and people.[11] In Luke's narrative of the encounter between Peter and Cornelius (in the Acts of the Apostles), it is shown that service conducted on behalf of another can change that person as well as the one who engages in the service, as Cornelius is changed through Peter's mediation yet Peter's view of the gentiles also has been changed. In other words, humble and helpful behavior helps not just those directly involved but also others within society. Through this type of behavior, a person can develop the capacity to recognize themselves more fully and be able to openly display their true self to others. In doing so, this person develops their capacity to comprehend their faith through new perspectives. When a Christian engages in a fundamental display of faith, other people are more inclined to respond.[12]

Religious Pluralism, Dialogue, and Mission

In the contemporary age, it is clear that Christianity is not alone in its effort to reach new hearts and minds. Almost every modern religion practices evangelism, using different strategies dependent upon adherents' beliefs, technological abilities, cultural contexts, and geographic locations. Simple street preachers can find themselves in direct competition with aggressive, and in some cases militant, international evangelism organizations. In the face of these opposing efforts, one could argue that interreligious dialogue should be regarded as one of the most important components of the church's mission.[13]

According to Centre for Global Leadership Development's Anand Sukhadeo Deshbhratar, the very purpose of interreligious dialogue is to contribute to the building of a community of freedom, coexistence, and equality.[14] This is a new and modern context for the church, an organization still influenced by a history in which some Christian mission activities were influenced by (or in

---

10. "Religious Plurality," 7.
11. "Religious Plurality," 11.
12. Rivera, *Political Theology and Pluralism*, 61.
13. Deshbhratar, "Missions and Religious Pluralism," 7.
14. Deshbhratar, 8.

some cases, directly connected to) matters of colonialism. Some see these past behaviors as having contributed to the destruction of peoples and cultures.[15] Through the same lens, belief in God calls us to a new and more intense form of mission activity: not to convert the entire world to our specific faith but to connect the world together in relationship.[16]

According to Marjorie Hewitt Suchocki's work regarding mission in a diversifying world, the central tasks of mission must be to share who we are, build relationships with one another, and learn to love one another.[17] In this context, Suchoki defines "friends" as people with whom we share something in common despite our mutual differences.[18] At the congregational level, interreligious dialogue can deepen one's faith: it does not require that either "friend" shed their identity and become the other, but that either "friend" offers themselves to the other and show willingness to work with the other toward the common good.[19]

In that context, friendship as a global mission is not only the building of relationships but also the seeking and clarification of knowledge:[20] knowledge of one another, of course, but also knowledge of wider notions. An honest exchange regarding the roots of societal ills that plague our planet, or the difficult histories faced by other groups of people, has the power to bring us together – especially if these harsh matters are lovingly discussed through the lenses of cultural and religious understanding. Conversion is not the goal: according to Marjorie Suchocki, "compassion is the mission."[21]

I agree with Alister E. McGrath, a doctrinal lecturer at Oxford University, that much of the uniqueness of Christianity lies within its doctrine of the Trinity.[22] Within our faith's framework, it is difficult to consider Jesus yet another religious figure among many others; Christ's unique qualities and divine nature clearly indicate that – within Christianity – he acts as the incarnation of God.[23] The evangelical reaction to interreligious dialogue has therefore affirmed that this dialogue must be free from the constraints of

---

15. Norris, "Mission and Religious Pluralism," 19.
16. Suchocki, *Divinity and Diversity*, 109.
17. Suchocki, 109.
18. Suchocki, 111.
19. Suchocki, 115.
20. Suchocki, 115.
21. Suchocki, 116.
22. See McGrath, "Christian Church's Response," 487–501.
23. McGrath, 488.

religious and cultural assumptions or stereotypes, as not all evangelicals are saying the same things.[24]

The distinct attributes of Christianity, when reinforced by the lessons bestowed upon the faith's adherents, indicate that finding common ground with others is an imperative of our religious belief. In finding common ground, we support the concept of pluralism. Commitment to Christian doctrine will lead us to engage in a real dialogue with non-Christians, helping us to generate new ways of cooperating with one another and to institute pro-dialogue internal reform – a necessity for common action.[25]

One could argue that ongoing pluralism is quite a challenge due to differing, and often oppositional, theological beliefs. Pluralism is deeply connected to the subject of coexistence, a system in which people can live together regardless of their agreements or differences. When theological or ideological differences begin to negatively impact the system of coexistence, conflict is the next logical step. The essence of pluralism is coexistence: when one learns to live with another person's differences, peace becomes possible.[26]

Another challenge of pluralism is the language of dialogue. We must approach one another in an apologetic and conciliatory manner, employing a compassionate attitude in the context of our search for friendship. We seek to understand "the other" and respect his or her doctrine.[27] As coexistence develops, it has the capacity to spread beyond basic societal issues: its supporters become advocates for the protection of the marginalized and the oppressed, and they work to empower those negatively impacted by societal ills. The community is empowered and becomes one that seeks justice and stability.[28]

Pluralism is a matter beyond ideological and theological debate: it is a process with the capacity to sidestep or overcome arguments between theologically divergent groups, different social classes, opposing ethnic groups, and those of otherwise separate political motivations. If conducted in an inclusive manner, with a focus on integrating the values of equality and justice, this effort of pluralism has the potential to greatly benefit its host society. Pluralism is a positive ethic that confirms the concept that "we are all

---

24. McGrath, 490.
25. McGrath, 492.
26. Mathewes, *Theology of Public Life*, 108.
27. Mathewes, 116.
28. Bradstock and Russell, "Politics," 171.

responsible for all" – a system in which collective social action takes the place of cultural individualism, and all benefit from this change.[29]

Religious Freedom and Coexistence

It is important to recognize the deep connections between religious freedom and coexistence. Pluralism is the essence of coexistence, and religious freedom stands as a solid and fundamental basis for contemporary efforts to enact coexistence. In this same context, religious evangelism has the potential to threaten the stability of a society engaged in coexistence-based efforts. Considering this matter, the evangelical figures responsible for the Lausanne Movement's Cape Town Commitment declared their position poignantly in their call to action:

> Upholding human rights by defending religious freedom is not incompatible with following the way of the cross when confronted with persecution. There is no contradiction between being willing personally to suffer the abuse or loss of our own rights for the sake of Christ, and being committed to advocate and speak up for those who are voiceless under the violation of their human rights. We must also distinguish between advocating the rights of people of other faiths and endorsing the truth of their beliefs. We can defend the freedom of others to believe and practise their religion without accepting that religion as true.
>
> A) Let us strive for the goal of religious freedom for all people. This requires advocacy before governments on behalf of Christians *and* people of other faiths who are persecuted.
>
> B) Let us conscientiously obey biblical teaching to be good citizens, to seek the welfare of the nation where we live, to honour and pray for those in authority, to pay taxes, to do good, and to seek to live peaceful and quiet lives. The Christian is called to submit to the state, unless the state commands what God forbids, or prohibits what God commands. If the state thus forces us to choose between loyalty to itself and our higher loyalty to God, we must say No to the state because we have said Yes to Jesus Christ as Lord.

---

29. Bradstock and Russell, 172.

> In the midst of all our legitimate efforts for religious freedom for all people, the deepest longing of our hearts remains that all people should come to know the Lord Jesus Christ, freely put their faith in him and be saved, and enter the kingdom of God.[30]

One of the main challenges to coexistence between people who follow different religions is related to the potential evangelistic mandates of those religions – that is, the religious goal of a faith's practitioners to attract additional followers to adhere to their own religiously mandated doctrines, practices, and ethics. Religious beliefs can differ widely, including a religion's general worldview, view of the divine, and perspective on the relationship between God and humanity. This creates a number of problems related to the matter of coexistence, ones that are especially relevant to the Middle East's Christian and Islamic faiths. To address it in a straightforward fashion: should we sacrifice evangelism or *da'wah* for the sake of coexistence? Should we sacrifice coexistence for the sake of evangelism or *da'wah*?

Evangelism and *da'wah* are the means by which the Christian and Islamic religions have expanded and spread to new geographical areas and populations, but – in some cases – this expansion can come at the cost of peaceful coexistence between followers of faiths, especially from those practitioners of faiths with deep historical roots in a given geographic or historic region. It is effectively impossible to eliminate or reduce the practices of evangelism and *da'wah*, since both are central to the core doctrines of both Christianity and Islam. Practically speaking, neither religion would have developed into their contemporary forms – or possess their respective modern-day influence – if not for the practices of evangelism and *da'wah*. As a result, these practices of "expanding the umbrella" of a given religion are considered essential, so much so that neither faith would likely give up on them at any future point.

What, then, should be done? Furthermore, how should we approach this theological and sociological issue? In my opinion, religious freedom is the best solution to this issue. When I speak of a "solution," I refer to the option that I believe has the best capacity to guarantee peaceful coexistence and ensure the creation of a free space in which people can choose, and practice, their religion.

However, religious freedom is lacking in many different regions of the world. As religiously minded people, what should we do about this? It is my sincere belief that we must continue to call for religious freedom, especially during this era in which it is lacking. We cannot stop talking about the

---

30. Third Lausanne Congress, *Cape Town Commitment*, IIC.6, 51.

importance of religious freedom: it is an essential element for the establishment of a peaceful and pluralistic society that accepts "otherness." It is not an easy path to walk, but to ensure the safety and prosperity of all, it is imperative that we remain committed to the tenets of religious freedom.

I now posit a follow-up question, to emphasize this important issue: how can a society achieve and sustain an ideal like religious freedom? Sociologists have long suggested different approaches to this concern, but many agree on the basic principle that plurality should be achieved within the social and cultural contours of a society before an attempt is made to institute such ethics with regards to religious practice. If the members of a society perceive that society is a safe space for "otherness," that society has the capacity to develop its own path toward religious freedom.

One can conclude that the model of the church's mission in the Christian context is the holistic model, where social responsibility – developmental efforts, religious freedom, political participation, and evangelism – are connected and complimentary. In general contexts, social responsibility and evangelism are separate missions and they work independently of one another. The church must act as a religious institution, where its commitments to human rights and the dignity of all peoples are realized. The church should also aim to practice the holistic model when this is possible, while still contributing to the promotion of social matters such as community peace and coexistence. There is no doubt, however, that there are increased challenges in communities with multiple religious denominations and/or cultures. In that context, different models may have different relevance.

In the context of transparency and involvement, the second model (which aligns with interpretation 3b, as presented in chapter 2) states that social responsibility is an independent mission to be accompanied by a transparent agenda and a commitment to coexistence. Peaceful existence is a goal in itself, and it deserves the attention of faith-based organizations and religious institutions. One can conclude that the second and the third models are both required efforts for the church, and the church can practice the third model, that of holistic mission, when it is productive to do so. Despite the presence of holistic mission, a transparent and credible model of social responsibility should be promoted by the church – either by itself, as a registered institution, or through an affiliated faith-based organization that is credible, committed, and transparently possessing no secondary agenda. Within the second model (3b), social responsibility is a mission in and of itself; the church can practice its holistic mission where it is possible, but it can also practice social responsibility in a non-theological fashion.

4

Evolution of Developmental Action

A Shift from Charity toward Social Resilience-Based Development

The matter of Egyptian development depends on the hands and minds of communities, and the success of such development is contingent upon a community's self-consciousness and recognition of its needs. The changing of the status quo is the overriding objective of any dedicated community development endeavour, but this goal is not accomplished just through theory and planning; dozens of hurdles must be cleared before any development agenda is to be brought into realization. These hurdles include poor community infrastructure, lack of access to human development opportunities (including educational and health services), long-standing traditions of dependence and hierarchy that undermine the spirit of initiative (entrepreneurship), the negative effects of myriad discriminatory practices that impact large swathes of the population, a universal sense of frustration and demoralization generated by exceptionally demanding international conditions, material resource constraints, and the delicate nature of the nascent Egyptian economy – an entity that, in my opinion, must be nurtured in its current state of infancy.

Long before a clear conceptualization of human development was developed on the international level – and prior to the discussion of this concept in different genres of literature and among separate cultures – some political doctrines indicated that the development of peoples could only be achieved through that people's hands, brains, and actions. This perception is further underscored by a globally uniform definition of human development, a concept that has been systematized in a sustained manner throughout the years and over different stages.

The Evolution of Conceptual Understanding of Development Action in Egypt
Stage 1: The Concept of Philanthropy and Charity

The notion of charitable work is premised on the assumption that disadvantaged and impoverished segments of society should have access to social welfare assistance. This value is considered by most to be imperative and fundamental, as there is no society at present that is relatively free from this trend – nor is any single society entirely spared from the reality of the presence of the poor and impoverished. Some examples of social welfare assistance include direct and frequent financial grants, the provision of shelter and food to the disadvantaged, and free access to health care and medical services.

Systemic charity in Egypt has a long legacy and is broadly defined to include channeling support to the country's citizens on an individual basis. This assistance, whether provided to the individual or the community, varies in substance and context: health care and medical services are among the most essential and are often paired with accommodative support for necessities (food and clothing). Educational supports – the construction of schools and the subsidization of a school student's financial demands – are also of paramount necessity. Other forms of prominent charitable work include the various aspects of crisis-based humanitarian relief and the offering of emergency assistance to populations that require immediate aid. In general, these services are delivered to disadvantaged populations: those vulnerable to the threat of poverty, hunger, illness, or displacement from their living quarters.

The concept of charity evolved over time, shifting away from the practice of individual engagement with the inception of a new institutional response model. The first charity to employ this tactic, the Greek Society in Alexandria, was founded in 1821 by the Greek community in that Mediterranean city. This event was quickly followed by the establishment of further associations, some cultural or academic in nature. Such efforts included the Egyptian Society for Research in the History of Egyptian Civilization (founded in 1859), the Egyptian Knowledge Society (founded in 1868), and the Egyptian Geographical Society (founded in 1875). Other associations of a religious character soon joined them, including the Islamic Charity Association (founded in 1878) and the Coptic Charity Association (founded in 1881).[1] It is worth noting that the latter half of the eighteenth century was marked by the formalization and institutionalization of philanthropic and charitable action as conducted through this wide spectrum of associations.

There was significant growth in the numbers of charities during the first three decades of the twentieth century. An example of this was Egypt's premier public university, King Fouad I University (now known as Cairo University), which was initially founded and funded on a pro-bono basis. Burgeoning civil society and charitable associations continued to flourish and grow, as supported by the formal recognition of the Egyptian rights of assembly and association, as enshrined under Article No. 30 of the Egyptian Constitution of 1923. The number of philanthropic and community-based associations increased exponentially. While 159 such organizations were formally registered by 1900, over four hundred new charities became operational (and recognized by the state) over the next two decades. By 1924, approximately 623 associations operated with the approval of the Egyptian government.[2]

Among the notable public figures engaged in such charitable work was King Farouk I, who had arrived from Britain in 1936 and acted as Egypt's head of state from 1936 to 1952. He worked philanthropically with multiple organizations, including the Islamic Mouwasat Association in Alexandria and Egypt's Tawfik Association. In 1939, he established the Ministry of Social Affairs, a department mandated to support the nationwide delivery of welfare and social services. In 1946, he went on to initiate the creation of an ad-hoc governmental council entrusted with the responsibility to combat poverty, illiteracy, and illness, as well as to defend and reinforce the rights of disadvantaged populations.

The central focus of philanthropic effort is to create a constructive response to current or ongoing societal needs. The magnitude of these needs that are often endemic within a society, or impacted by matters well outside of a single citizen group's control, is far beyond the capacity and capability of these associations, however. The entities that commit to the charitable approach proceed from the assumption that, by directing a little aid to the unprivileged groups of population, these groups will be capable of "getting back on their feet" and will no longer require additional aid. On the contrary, hands-on

---

1. Gaiyed, "Nash't Al-Jam'yat Al-A'hlyya," accessed 25 Nov 2020, http://coptcatholic.net/p4256/.

2. Shoe'ir, "Al Jam'eyat Al-Ahlyh" accessed 25 Nov 2020, http://www.ahewar.org/debat/show.art.asp?aid=540096.

experience indicates that target communities provided with exorbitant degrees of systemic assistance often find themselves dependent upon this assistance. Related to this issue is the fact that such aid is usually based on a temporary relief scheme, intended to address the outward manifestations of poverty rather than its causal factors.

Central to the criticism of such work is the idea that the aforementioned temporary solutions will actually contribute to the creation of new problems and have a negative impact upon long-term development efforts. For the most part, this approach elicits the "relief dependency syndrome" – the belief that aid work creates a certain level of reliance among the targeted groups, and that long-term altruistic work is not sustainable. Notwithstanding this criticism, the methodology behind this temporary relief-based charitable work fits well with the philanthropic position of the clerical communities, which promote charity and philanthropy as expressions of the social welfare role of their respective religious institution – a function that has been received with much reservation from those individuals with conservative leanings.

Stage 2: Community Development in Egypt

Community development is described as the "post-charity" phase. Promoting attention to, or demonstrating interest in, the matter of local development at the community level is a long-standing social practice, well-regulated under social systems and monitored by most countries of the world to ensure that development efforts adhere to sound principles. Therefore, many governments have established departments for local development that report to the relevant coordinative governmental departments responsible for developmental and social affairs. This allows for these social partners to follow up on the quality of life of individuals, identify adverse factors and grassroots-based challenges, and recommend appropriate solutions to either mitigate the impact of these factors on society or address their root causes in a holistic manner. This evolved and overarching concept of community development coalesced in the 1970s. Its adherents, many at the local level, maintained a focus on the delivery of social welfare services while also attending to long-term developmental and societal matters. It is essential to underscore the fact that grassroots-level development represents the nerve center of human development in any human society, especially developing societies.

Local development refers to political, social, and economic efforts by a population group that lives in a specific geographic area. These efforts are also undertaken in order to foster a sense of social unity via the promotion of the prevailing value system, which the local development efforts act to supplement. The parameters and components of a community, along with its hallmark features, may be determined on the basis of criteria including geographic boundaries, demographics, mutually dependent relationships at the community level, shared social systems and relationships, patriotic sentiments, feelings of loyalty and belonging toward a non-kin group, community-based inter-group interactions, a group self-consciousness among community members, and other general shared values and standards. These factors contribute to the creation of a community's cultural identity and emotional unity, which coalesce into entities such as "cities," "villages," "neighborhoods," and other population centers. This systemic view of local development underscores the idea that the community is not a free-standing unit but rather a thread within a broad and complex social fabric.

Despite divergent views on the concept of local community, there is consensus among promoters of different interpretations about certain fundamental points which should be taken into consideration within the context of community-focused studies and/or community development efforts. For instance, most believe that it is important to identify the geographical and ecological conditions that distinguish one local community from the other, and to assess the extent to which these conditions impact the community's economic and demographic conditions. In addition, conducting research on the psychological/psycho-social dimension of a community is of paramount importance to the process of successful developmental change. The complex reality of social relationships must be taken into consideration when examining local development, as it will lead to knowledge of the nature, classifications, and social stratification of coexisting community groups.

Consequently, local community development can be described as a process of undertaking a suite of interventions and functional activities to achieve overall progress in the community. It may also be defined as promotion of specific behaviors and codes of conduct, or sharpening the skills and competencies of individual community members so that they can further develop themselves, thus producing a net positive impact within the community in a manner that leads to additional growth across many institutional and societal sectors.

Community development involves the modification of relationship dynamics between ordinary people and people in positions of power, so that everyone can have a say in the issues that affect their lives. The role of citizens in their own community is not solely limited to performing in their jobs or occupations, but also involves engagement in matters of interest to them. Community development stems from the principle that, within any community, there is a wealth of knowledge and experience which – if used creatively – can be channeled into collective action to achieve a community's desired goals. Community development requires a modality of cooperation between diverse members of the same community so that it can have a chance to impact economic, social, and cultural aspects. One of the natural benefits of community development is shifting centralized management to a more decentralized model – one in which local figures, those directly exposed to and engaged in local matters, have more power over local issues. Therefore, community development seeks to reinforce the mandate of localities and community development institutions in promoting local development and ensuring that all associated activities are performed to the best benefit of the target community.

Several recent concepts of development have emerged from international and intra-national sources. One of particular interest is the new concept of development espoused by the United Nations. The United Nations defines community development as "a process where community members and the government come together to take collective action and generate solutions to common problems."[3] These efforts are undertaken in order to improve various economic, social, cultural, and environmental aspects of communities, typically aiming to contribute to the advancement of the country as much as possible. Economic development can be achieved through a policy mandating state ownership of means of production or through a free market policy adopted by capitalist countries.

A number of different approaches to community development can be recognized and put into use simultaneously. The concept of "development" contains a wide array of tried-and-true sub-focuses, and includes matters ranging from community economic development (CED) and community capacity building to social capital formation, ecologically sustainable development, and asset-based community development. Although the benchmarks and indicators of development are many and diverse, there is consensus that the overarching goal of economic development is to provide a life of dignity to citizens, ensure social well-being, and promote the values of justice and equality.

With this goal in mind, there are three aspects that must be taken into consideration when establishing development benchmarks or standards. These aspects are as follows:

---

3. UN, "Community Development."

- economic growth
- environmental quality
- human relationships

On the basis of its various definitions, the concept of "development" can be further summed up in three major trends. The first trend concludes that development is synonymous with social welfare; however, this is based on a narrow and strict definition of the concept of welfare. The second trend considers development to be a range of social services that are delivered in several fields, such as health care and education. Development is defined as a dynamic process of transformation on three different tiers:

1. *Transformation of individuals* in order to affirm faith in their ability to alter reality, engage in collective action, and generate interest in achievement based on scientific foundations.

2. *Transformation of the social structure and its functions* in order to reduce the divide between the social classes, facilitate social mobility, preserve justice in distribution of wealth and incomes, and broaden the economic space and ensure diversification of economic activities against the backdrop of decentralized and democratic/democratizing institutions.

3. *Transformation of community's relationship with the outside world* with an aim to achieve political autonomy and economic liberalization to reach equal trade relations with the nations of the world while maintaining cultural specificities, encouraging adaptation and localization of indigenous technology, and adopting a selective approach toward advanced technology. These aspects have the objective of satisfying the rapidly changing (and ever-expanding) interests of individuals within the community. This may be done only through a social revolution as initiated/directed by the state.

The third trend perceives social development to be a process of social change originating from within the social structure and its functionaries (such as institutions), with an aim to accommodate the social needs of individuals and groups alike. In this trend, social development is a process of social change that is brought about in a traditional setting. Thus, establishing new social structures will give rise to new relationships and new values that satisfy the interests, needs, and aspirations of individuals within the community. Toward this end, a major communal effort is needed to bring about qualitative changes and achieve the envisaged progress.[4]

The Concepts of Growth and Development

The perception of growth differs from that of development. Within the modern complex, growth can sometimes involve the possibility of exploitation; in this sense, growth can be lopsided or unbalanced. It can be parasitic in nature, and thus prejudicial to surrounding individuals, entities, and institutions. In contrast, development in its true meaning involves equilibrium, inclusiveness, and equality. Development in its full sense is based on an "accumulative build-up" model: both qualitative and quantitative in nature, this practice entails no exploitation of an entity at the expense of another.

The concept of "growth" refers to constant or continued gains achieved in a certain aspect of life, while "development" involves a rapid increase over a specific period of time. In other words, "growth" occurs through slow-paced evolution and gradual transformation, while "development" accounts for a strong (and perhaps sudden) boost that can help a society emerge from a state of social or economic recession. This strong boost is the reverse of gradual negative transformation. Change that is driven by growth is insignificant as it is slow and not geared toward changing environmental structures, while change that is obtained through development addresses the structural and functional aspects of life – in other words, it is change that is more qualitative than quantitative in nature.[5]

Whilst the first half of the twentieth century was marked by a shift from the notion of charity to the concept of development, the second half of the twentieth century included a shift toward new concepts of development, specifically those of a comprehensive and sustainable nature.

Inclusive Development

Inclusive development involves all those meaningful processes that are geared toward the generation of society-wide social and economic progress. Achieving such a goal, however, requires consistent contribution, participation, and feedback from the local community. Inclusive development seeks to give focus to all vulnerabilities in a given society, whether economic, political,

---

4. Al-Samaloṭi, *'elm Ejtmaʿ Al-Tanmya*, 119.
5. Ḥassan, *Al-Tanmya Al-Ejtmaʿyya*, 95.

or social. The internal and external forces combined lend themselves to the progress and development achieved in different spheres and seek to address such vulnerabilities. In addition, they seek to unleash the dormant potential of individuals by means of opening up avenues of creativity and innovation.

Inclusive development serves as a means to help individuals escape the clutches of poverty and overcome unemployment by creating job opportunities. In addition, inclusive development concerns itself with the achievement of justice and equality in the distribution of national wealth, the right to freedom of expression, the defeat of illiteracy, and the empowerment of individuals to participate in decision-making. Its focus on the whole range of aspects of the lives of individuals is the reason it is labelled as inclusive development.

It may be concluded therefore that inclusive development is an integrated process aimed at generating a combination of structural transformations by directing and leveraging individuals' conscious efforts through stimulating their productive capacity.[6]

Sustainable Development

The concept of "sustainable development" was first promoted in 1987 as part of the World Commission on Environment and Development's *Our Common Future* report. Sustainable development is a broad developmental concept that concerns itself with tackling interlinked crises facing the greater human civilization. This concept involves three essential concepts: (1) economic development, (2) social justice, (3) and environmental protection.

The concept of sustainable development was recognized and adopted universally at the Earth Summit held by the World Commission on Environment and Development in 1992. An important anchor within the 1992 Rio Declaration, it gained further prominence through its inclusion in certain operational frameworks and programs of action promoted by the United Nations (such as Agenda 21). In 1993, the Commission on Sustainable Development was founded as an effort of the United Nations General Assembly – the highest existing international inter-governmental body, representing the governments of member states engaging in efforts to address international resolutions as associated with the agenda of the twenty-first century (Agenda 21). Later, these programs were further developed into a more realistic framework: the Johannesburg Plan of Implementation, first introduced to the United Nations' member countries at the Earth Summit held in Johannesburg in 2002. The

---

6. ESCWA, *Comprehensive Social Development Report*.

Commission on Sustainable Development was entrusted with the mandate of following up on the execution of the Johannesburg Plan, and it was also charged with the responsibility of ensuring the adherence of all states and parties involved to the requirements of these programs.

Prior to these efforts, the United Nations had engaged in a degree of initiatives aimed at addressing both the economic and ecological ills of its subsidiary nations. In 1972, for instance, the United Nations General Assembly created the United Nations Environment Program. This entity was empowered to launch and promote practical mechanisms to better direct and organize the essential environmental and development activities of the United Nations. In 1988, the United Nations General Assembly established the Intergovernmental Panel on Climate Change (IPCC), an independent body dedicated to monitor climate change issues; the panel contributed to the drafting of the Kyoto Protocol, a well-regarded international environmental action plan that has successfully led to reduction of global greenhouse gas emissions since its introduction in 2005.

In 2008, the United Nations Environment Program introduced the Green Economy Initiative aimed at the formalization and centralization of sustainable development efforts, specifically those focused on the elimination of poverty. In this context, the 2012 United Nations Conference on Sustainable Development – also known as Rio+20, as it took place in Rio de Janeiro – adopted as its primary themes the concept of "the green economy in the context of sustainable development and poverty eradication" and "an institutional framework for sustainable development."[7] In addition, the 2019 progress report of the United Nations Development Program (UNDP) raised a question directed at United Nations organs and sub-entities: "How do we commit to work?" Some of the suggestions communicated in reply to this question revolved around the need to develop sustainable solutions by "not doing business as usual," by providing intellectual leadership, and by taking a leading role in the defense of humanitarian causes.[8]

---

7. UN, "Green Economy," United Nations Conference," accessed 25 Nov 2020, https://sustainabledevelopment.un.org/topics/greeneconomy.

8. Chuma, "Employment"; Luomi et al., *Arab Region SDG Index*; Hujaila and Rafika, "Development."

Evolution of Inclusive and Sustainable Development Strategies

In order to succeed in establishing inclusive and sustainable development, it has proven essential for those engaged in the agenda of development and developmentally oriented strategies to evolve in their methodology. Community-based development strategies changed over time, shifting away from the delivery of direct services intended to meet the needs of the community and toward fostering partnerships with civil society organizations (CSOs) at the grass roots level. Within this model, the CSOs serve as developmental intermediaries empowered to manage the development programs; they are supplemented in this effort by the work of those within the governmental sector and the entities representing the private business community. This has led to the introduction of a rights-based approach to development: an approach to community change that is founded on the principles of human rights such as equality, accountability, transparency, and participation. Additionally, a special emphasis has been placed on the engagement and empowerment of rights holders in communities by ensuring that they can organize themselves. These rights holders, once joined together into community groups, have the capacity to support and advocate for their own interests and uphold their rights – thus having a positive bearing on their community's social and economic conditions.

The generation and adoption of the social resilience-based development model also increased the repertoire of those engaged in development. This school of developmental thought is geared toward capacity building and resource mobilization as effective means by which to confront existing risks, threats, and challenges. Special efforts are taken to employ training and better inform communities of economic and social "best practices," in order to promote a "projective perspective" to better identify and prepare for anticipated risks and changes.

In the early 1960s, a strategic approach to participatory development was introduced. According to the tenets of this model, young development practitioners from target communities were required to reach out to local citizens in order to better seek information and identify the needs and problems of a community via participatory activism. With this information, development practitioners had a better capacity to explore ways of providing essential services to citizens of different groups and geographic areas. Matters such as urban social welfare, family planning, health services, and education were discussed with citizens in the cities, while issues such as the roles of women in society, the agricultural industry, and the distribution of livestock and poultry were addressed in rural villages. This approach further evolved in the following years to encompass new sectors such as environmental protection, shelter and housing needs, economic development within multiple industries, and a variety of other more precise development programs.

In the 1980s and 1990s, the field of development continued to evolve with the introduction of the self-reliance strategy (SRS). The primary focus of this approach was on the development of services, community development, and capacity/training development as defined and requested by the communities themselves. Through direct participation in the development process, individuals and groups began to develop the capacity to influence the responses and solutions to the very issues that impacted their livelihoods. This approach has further matured, leading to greater favourable changes with special consideration being given to the democratic empowerment of community leaders and grassroots institutions to ensure sustained change.

At the dawn of the third millennium, the strategies for action further changed with the times. Moving away from the participatory and self-reliance models, the developmental field began to adopt the capacity-building approach (CBA). More experienced and wide-scale development organizations began to assume the role of umbrella organizations with a specific mandate to undertake development endeavors. These efforts were undertaken expressly for the benefit of local communities and were supported through continuously strengthened partnerships with local grassroots intermediaries and existing or newly founded community-based development organizations (CBOs). The CBA was not the only new development methodology introduced during this period, however. Under the institutional support approach, modalities of grant financing have been enacted to endorse the capacity of local CBOs to independently participate in the practice of development and create their own models of effective community engagement. By decentralizing development activities, these organizations could more specifically address the identified problems and needs of local citizens in different areas that have a bearing on development – issues including all aforementioned matters as well as new emphases on women's empowerment, cultural issues, working children, and the necessity of resisting prejudicial practices. In addition to the institutional capacity building of local CBOs, a number of new interventions were employed to strengthen and encourage the autonomous organization of local advocacy groups to address key areas of concern.

As we surveyed these different positions regarding development, we now come to explain in detail how each approach develops the concept of development itself.

Rights-Based Approach

The first decade of the third millennium witnessed the evolution of a new strategy: the "rights-based" approach to development. This new approach was based upon the following ideals:

- The target populations must be treated as full-fledged citizens, responsible for every duty and entitled to every right. They are defined as "rights holders."
- Citizens must be fully included and engaged. Marginalized and underprivileged populations, whether individually or in groups, should be connected to governmental and public systems to better enable them to access all the services they need through relevant service providers (described as "duty bearers").
- Marginalized and excluded populations should be allowed and empowered to organize themselves, to become more acquainted with their own rights, to develop their capacity to advocate for those rights, and to access their rights. Advocacy is a key mechanism to bring about change, develop impoverished communities, and pursue essential reforms of legal procedures and governmental policy frameworks. These efforts can only succeed with continuing assistance from a third group, known as "rights supporters." These are the people who are convinced of these rights and support their achievement.

Within the context of the rights-based approach, special consideration should be given to the empowerment of all poor and marginalized populations at the community level. Those engaged in developmental work should act to enable these groups to organize themselves, strengthen their capacities to work and communicate with each other, work closely alongside them, and endorse further additional democratic initiatives. With this type of support, citizens may join together in different community-based organizations such as democratically elected committees (ECs), which are public nongovernmental bodies in which citizens are able to organize themselves by electing their representatives in free elections, and where citizens become key agents in their own change process and are no longer perceived as mere service recipients. Furthermore, the rights holders must believe and promote the ideal that development is a human right, while duty bearers need to appreciate the fact that they are under an obligation to fulfill specific duties and responsibilities for the benefit of citizens.

To ensure success within the rights-based model, it is essential to embrace these foundational concepts and principles while also securing consent from all parties involved. Matters of agreement must include the reciprocal relationship between human rights, democracy, and development – a triad that, within this framework, forms a mutually beneficial and reciprocal relationship. Likewise, it is important to recognise the fact that citizen participation is not a means to an end but rather a developmental goal in its own right. To espouse the principle of "collective force" and enable citizens to act as rights holders – those who can develop a solid foundation from which to demand their lost or sought rights – will, in turn, allow them to eventually address the needs of their own community in an independent manner. Disempowerment is one of the causes of poverty and impoverishment, and perhaps among the main reasons behind the high prevalence of community violence, intolerance, prejudice, and partiality. If managed properly, the empowerment of community groups can lead to distinct improvement of living conditions among poor and marginalized populations. These efforts must also be employed in tandem with the reinforcement of confidence-building and dialogue between the state and its citizens, as well as efforts to promote collaborative work, a social culture of peace, and social cohesion.

Territorial Approach to Local Development (TALD)

In addition to the rights-based developmental model, the territorial approach to local development (TALD) began to be practiced at the same time. This approach focuses on the interlinked relationships between endogenous, integrated, multi-scalar, and incremental local development efforts.

The TALD approach was introduced in response to recognition of significant disparity between characteristics and qualities of food and non-food agricultural products across various rural areas. This concern led to the formation of advocacy groups that represented the interests of producers, consumers, intermediaries, and other related segments of society. These groups, referred to as "stakeholders," were directly interested in working together to promote the continuity of the local product's quality as well as (potentially) the product's improvement.

This approach was reinvigorated with the rise of globalization among European Union (EU) countries. Its member nations struggled to maintain their competitiveness across various areas (particularly the economic sector) under constantly shifting global conditions, which by nature represent a threat to the survival of "weaker players," such as countries with developing economies. Prior to the application of TALD, the "power players" – Western nations with developed economies – were the only horses able to stand on the racetrack. Quickly, the very techniques utilized to reinforce the power of those "power players" would go on to be used as part of globalized development efforts.

Globalization contributed to the "lost decade of development" via international policies that supplemented the economic status quo at the expense and disadvantage of developing nations. At the same time, these developing nations – still negatively affected by policies that reinforced the strength of the "power players" – had to engage with challenges associated with quality of life, quality of food, and food security. This stimulated an earnest search for new approaches to development – models that, if employed widely and locally, could provide benefits to not just developing nations but also marginalized territories within the developed world. During this time frame, the 1980s and 1990s, social and political frictions in several countries' restive regions boiled over into civil war or intra-national conflict – further endorsement that serious consideration should be given to approaches that prioritize such territories/regions in order to afford them the opportunity to escape from the web of deprivation and destitution.

Within this context, the term "territory" is defined as any social, economic, and political entity or structure that maintains an identity that has been formed on the basis of common experiences and collective action, as strengthened by the underpinnings of intra-social competition. This structure or entity is capable of mobilizing actors who hold a common interest and who can be organized through advocacy institutions within the concerned territory. If joined together in a synergy of efforts with other entities or structures on different levels in its geographic proximity (local, regional/provincial, national, etc.), these actors have the capacity to engage in a type of local development that is endogenous, integrated, and multi-scalar.

TALD, therefore, is defined as a suite of complex, intertwined value-additive operations that make the most of existing human and natural resources, whether exhaustible, material, or immaterial (e.g., a group of actors who have a shared interest in a fixed economic or social asset), on the basis of collective action (social, economic, or political). This approach is *endogenous* as it employs local actors to make the most of the available resources. It is also *integrated* because of the model's emphasis on coordinating the work of different institutions in a given territory (and thus avoiding sectoral fragmentation of development interventions). Finally, TALD is also *multi-scalar* – possessing mechanisms to allow for cooperation at different levels – and *incremental*, seeking to multiply its desired impact.⁹

The territorial approach to local development capitalizes on the collective action of groups of actors or constituencies with shared interests that are inextricably interwoven in a flexible geographic framework, leading to the cumulation of experiences and expertise needed to produce a product of a special quality and "identity." TALD is highly participatory. In addition, this methodology can reinforce the impact of other spatial development models, thus acting synergistically with other approaches to development and not inconsistently with any one of them; on the contrary, TALD can make the most of other techniques and multiply their effects. This approach seeks to target multiple geographic territories, the selection of which is determined by the nature of common interest among the actors of the concerned agricultural-economic activity with an aim at increasing the competitiveness of this activity area. Within the TALD framework, for a territorial approach to be effective it must be congruent with the values, economic patterns, and social patterns of the target territory.

By applying this approach, we can reach out to flexible ("scalable") geographic regions or territories that are distinguished by hallmark features in a given agricultural or economic sector on the basis of shared interests of concerned actors. This involves the design and delivery of territorial initiatives that are aimed at enhancing the capacity of selected territories. These efforts are undertaken to establish or reinforce an economic system that is driven by competitive advantages and common interests. During this process, key actors concerned with the targeted agricultural-economic activities are brought together to work on issues. Thus, partnership-building opportunities and an increase in organizational/marketing capabilities of key actors, as well as, potentially, an increase in value (perceived or real) of target products, are positive side effects for participation in TALD efforts.¹⁰

Social Resilience Approach

Alongside the rights-based approach to development and the territorial approach to local development, the social resilience-based approach to development began to be practiced at the same time.

---

9. Bilbao, "What Is the Territorial Approach?"
10. Bilbao.

The social resilience-based approach is oriented toward efforts to increase the capacity and enhance the readiness of individuals, groups, and institutions to better enable them to manage, address, and cope with the current and projected threats through training, information development, and local cultural adjustment. It consists of four strategies: coping, adaptation, transformation, and social protection. Effectively, the purpose of this strategy is to build the resilience of individuals, groups, institutions, and communities to keep pace with current and future changes, and to enable them to effectively walk with their communities/constituencies toward more sustainable outcomes. These efforts are to be undertaken while also promoting a more inclusive, fair, and sustainable society for all participants.

The Concept of Resilience[11]
Although the concept has its origins in the field of ecological studies, the means by which people learn to cope with changes that occur in their environments (over many years, and in a world that is in constant social, economic, and political flux) has required the scope of such a general notion as "resilience" to be stretched to include many varied aspects. The concept has ballooned from an initially narrow definition – one that merely indicates the capacity of actors to respond to problems – to a directly related but infinitely more complex definition: the capacity of actors to learn, cope, and adapt to major issues.

The concept has been further broadened to include an individual's ability to participate in good governance operations and work toward the transformation of community structures, for the purpose of addressing emergent changes both on the local and global levels. The concepts of "strengths" and "resilience" involve key principles, including persistence, adaptability, and transformability. In addition, the concept has further evolved to signify the capacity of individuals, groups, households, communities, enterprises, and states to become more productive during times of stability as well as to cope, reorganize, and continue to prosper in response to times of unrest. Thus, within the context of the contemporary definition, the notion of resilience places more emphasis on the capacity of actors and less on the systems – more on the development of new capacities and practices, and less on functions.

In order to endorse system-wide resilience, the social resilience model endorses the enhancing of skills associated with the social resilience model within existing institutions and societal structures. These entities are

---

11. Information in this section drawn from Keck and Sakdaplrak, "What Is Social Resilience?," 5–19.

supplemented in their efforts by peer support networks at the local level, which assess citizens' needs through data set assessment, observe the implementation of social resiliency efforts, and systematically evaluate the outcomes of such efforts throughout each stage of delivery. In conducting multiple levels of review, the social resilience model – designed to attain sustainable and measurable outcomes – ensures as much feedback and assessment as possible.

In brief, the social resilience approach is a collective, skills-driven approach that is aimed at improving individual and collective well-being and resilience. This model seeks to address the tension between the current reality and projected future by teaching skills and competencies needed to increase engagement, modify trends brought on by a lack of organization, enhance persistence at the individual level, and promote creativity and innovation at the community level. The model makes use of collaborative intelligence within and across entities, doing so in a manner that promotes the interest of individuals and organizations alike. Ultimately, social resilience is concerned with the capacity of individuals to define what is perceived to be a threat or a disaster and what is not – an effective result of advocacy toward democratization.[12]

Core Values and Goals of the Social Resilience Approach to Development

As discussed at length, the potential benefits of the social resilience approach to local development are numerous, and its values are in line with contemporary Egypt. Citizens should have the ability to build creative and innovative capacities at all levels, develop a community's physiological self-awareness capacity during crises, tap into potential opportunities during periods of stability, promote "collaboration through diversity," and better enable participants to engage in collective capacity-building efforts. When employed proactively, this approach has shown itself capable of strengthening human capital and social assets, evolving continuously as a result of continued evaluation and modification, engaging social stakeholders at all levels, training and linking strategic actors across various entities (while also developing the leadership capacities of those actors), and promoting the natural human tendency toward resilience. These new social networks can go on to mainstream insightful visions and practices across training modules and structures – for instance, creating educational settings that are high quality, affordable, sustainable, scalable and replicable – as well as establishing additional relationships that ensure the dissemination and self-replication of the social resilience model with a focus on fostering peer collaboration and support. Such networks can leverage thorough and consistent

---

12. See Keck and Sakdapolrak, "What Is Social Resilience?," 5–19.

implementation of social resilience policies at the sectoral and governmental levels and promote assessments of these efforts' outcomes to subsequently inform future processes (through the use of "best practices"). Within the framework of the social resilience approach to development, society itself has the capacity to reinforce the rights of survival, respect, social participation, dignity of life, and access to a decent life for all of its participants.[13]

Therefore, the primary purpose of the social resilience approach to development is to build up the most vulnerable communities, institutions, and individuals through the enhancement of their resilience. These communities must be able to develop their readiness and preparedness, have their social cohesion fostered, and have their capacity to withstand and recover from crises bolstered. Vulnerable communities must be enabled to develop effective mechanisms that contribute to the overall resilience of their societies, so that they can cope with present and potential risks, shocks, threats, and changes in all economic, social, and climatic spheres. This must be accomplished alongside the confronting of poverty, efforts to improve the quality and security of life for the disadvantaged and marginalized, and fair access to sustainable and equitable development. In dedicating itself to these goals, a society has the ability to bring about justice, equality, and human dignity for all.

Facing the Future

We continue to navigate this insightful journey toward a future that is reinforced by sustained and impactful development efforts. Though these initiatives have contributed to an increase in the quality of life for needy and less privileged populations, research into the matter must continue, driven by a careful examination of successful and well-proofed developmental approaches, and always taking into account the changing natures of temporal, social, political, and cultural contexts faced not just by the local community but the universal human community.

It is essential to address the purpose of long-term sustainable development work, specifically those efforts developed and instituted as part of civil society. In the second chapter of this text, I discuss the matter of the kingdom of God, a phenomena occurring both now and at an inevitable future time, during which God's reign becomes manifest on earth. Different models of affecting societal change in alignment with the kingdom of God were observed. For instance, the second model (3b) – an approach that emphasizes the equally important yet

---

13. Greene, "Resilience," 526–531.

separate natures of Christ's social and evangelistic missions – was employed by Samuel Habib and has since proven to be an effective foundation for change. The very existence of the second model (3b) displays theological resilience. Reflectively applying the tenets of the Christian faith to contemporary problems allows for constructive and kingdom-led methodologies of social engagement to be developed, put to use, and redeveloped as necessary. The evolution of these models, emerging as a result of much time and effort spent putting them into effect, shows the survivability and validity of such work. The theological resilience of the kingdom's tenets is continuously reinforced through its ability to respond to emergent issues in today's world.

Keeping these factors in mind, it is thus possible to assess the efforts of civil society through the oft-applicable lens of the kingdom of God. Blessed with a "great banquet" (Luke 14:12–14) of skills and resources, non-governmental organizations have had the privilege of inviting the underprivileged to its table for kingdom-inspired nourishment. Training, advocacy, economic opportunities, and more forms of assistance are available as a result of biblically relevant virtues such as charity and respect. The second model (3b) allows for long-term developmental work to be enacted within the Egyptian context; yet it should also be noted that the third model (3c) could be utilized successfully by a religious institution, specifically in working with its own congregations and religious population.

I am convinced, however, that there are valid perspectives beyond theology by which one can assess social change; in many cases, these outwardly secular perspectives complement the aforementioned kingdom-led theological approach. The merits of "social mission" could be measured through a non-religious assessment of its capacity to positively impact the social and political settings in which such an effort is undertaken; after all, community developmental endeavors are undertaken by local agents of change to affect shifts inside an existing culture and society. Within certain environments, a purely theological approach to social action could, in fact, prevent the success of that mission.

5

Locally Based Initiatives

The Developmental Evolution of Coptic Evangelical Organization for Social Services (CEOSS)

Sustainable initiatives are not just a means to an end, an opportunity to provide situational aid, or an effort to temporarily "patch a hole" in society. On the contrary, community initiatives have the capacity to act as replicable models of change. If utilized correctly and reapplied to new social problems, these flexible models can be utilized to correct a number of societal issues while also building up supports that may prevent the issues from repeating or becoming worse over the years. Civil society organizations have the opportunity to take these models and use them to build resilient communities.

In their approach to development, theologically minded civil society organizations aim to contribute to positive change for the sake of Egyptian society, its citizens having been created in the image of God. When an agency builds up the capacity of affiliated non-governmental organizations, those partners become more able to assist and educate their fellow citizens; as a result, the everyday Egyptian is equipped to engage with civil society and becomes more resilient (both socially and politically) over time. Muslim or Christian, these increasingly empowered Egyptians are more likely to independently and sustainably enact social, political, and structural changes that impact their condition. Supported by efforts such as civil engagement and the formation of local councils, these advances are initiated and conducted by the communities themselves. As the society proves itself capable of supporting the "least of these" (Matt 25:40), the self-directed efforts of affiliated community organizations gradually replace charity work and direct outreach.

Community development endeavors also contribute to the maturation of a resilient society. As disadvantaged villages and informal urban areas begin to flourish through the institution of customized economic programs, local organizations such as farmers' cooperatives and business associations establish an atmosphere of development. Through training programs, Egyptians without formal vocational experience are given a "hand up" (as opposed to a "handout") toward employment, developing skills that can be passed on to other members of their communities. Large-scale local development efforts are able to shift from crisis response, and the provision of basic goods, to sustainable (and measurable) efforts that provide essential tools for long-term local prosperity. In short order, members of local communities are able to assist their economically disadvantaged brothers and sisters – doing so in a domestic and culturally sensitive manner that best suits local conditions. Step by step, the loving values of the kingdom of God become integrated into those of the greater society. With enough reinforcement, Egypt can develop a culture of social resilience, which, in turn, allows the ever-present kingdom of God to evolve and expand in righteous fashion.

A Brief History of CEOSS

Inspired by the models introduced in chapter 2 and chapter 3 of this text – especially the second model (3b) – the Egyptian Presbyterian Church was led in the 1950s to establish the Coptic Evangelical Organization for Social Services (CEOSS) as an agent of social change. This organization was created to carry on the concept of social mission, and as an independent mission, to serve all humans without any discrimination on the grounds of race, origin, or religious background.

CEOSS is an Egyptian non-profit organization that seeks to improve the quality of life of disenfranchised and impoverished local populations through community development, particularly in the spheres of the economy and health care. CEOSS makes every effort to disseminate and promote the values of justice, equality, and citizenship among residents of the local communities in which it works. CEOSS makes its services accessible to all Egyptian citizens, with no discrimination whatsoever on the grounds of gender, faith, or creed.

CEOSS embarked on its service mission in 1950 with its work in the field of literacy. In an earnest effort made by the late Rev. Dr. Samuel Habib, great efforts were taken to assist in the plight of those who struggle with illiteracy, poverty, and a lack of societal power in Nazlet Ḥaraz, a village in the Abu Qurqaṣ District of Minya Governorate. At that time, approximately 11.5 percent of the local population was literate; by 1954, the literacy rate in Nazlet Ḥaraz had increased to 24 percent.

As this pilot experience had proven to be successful, CEOSS continued to approach and pursue its mission with the same dedication, while acknowledging a growing sense of agency purpose. New programs of action were introduced, such as vocational and handicraft skills training, support for those involved in rural poultry farming and breeding, and the publication of the free educational newsletter *Resalat Al-Nour* (literally translated as "the message of light"). The purpose of this publication – the first of its kind in Egypt – was to provide post-literacy follow-up supports to the newly literate, in order to prevent their relapse into illiteracy.

An Evolving Development Agenda

Over time, the developmental agenda espoused by CEOSS evolved. Based on a careful analysis of the course of action pursued by the organization from its inception to the current day, it is evident that the philosophical underpinnings of the CEOSS-supported developmental paradigm have developed over time. Starting in the early 1950s, the late Rev. Dr. Samuel Habib set out to raise awareness of sound practices in the fields of health, farming, and education practices among farmers in small hamlets and villages of the Minya Governorate. This work had developed significantly by the 1980s, at which point CEOSS was designing and implementing large-scale local action plans to support development projects (in varying fields and requiring expertise in each) based on an understanding and assessment of the needs of local communities. By the end of the 1990s, CEOSS's target communities began to lead the process of their own needs' assessment, prioritization, and action plan recommendations. At this time, CEOSS was continuing to empower individual members of target communities and existing local development organizations, assisting them in acquiring and developing the skills they needed to support the achievement of goals and objectives.

In recent years, CEOSS has been able to successfully develop a broader understanding of the concept of "human development" and to translate this new comprehension into successful developmental endeavors that widely impact the diverse populations of Cairo's more disadvantaged neighborhoods. These modern development projects – whether in the streets, schools, community organizations, health-care clinics, or youth centers – have proven to be an effective means of enacting social change. Children have recovered from their illnesses due to better access to medical care, while disadvantaged women have developed the means to counteract oppression and combat injustice. Unemployed young people, previously occupied by a societal sense of arrested economic productivity, have had the ability to dedicate themselves instead to an income-generating craft or a successful business. After being able to contribute and engage with society, persons with special needs have proven to possess the ability to overcome hurtful labels and the insensitive designation of "disability." Local women and men have begun to speak the language of management and social responsibility, as they have successfully awakened their communities from a stagnant sleep that spanned years, or perhaps decades.

CEOSS's strategies of action have evolved from simply providing direct services that aim at fulfilling a community's immediate needs to a complex and decentralized multi-regional effort that includes partnership-building with grassroots civil society organizations (CSOs). This effort came as a result of the agency's continuous dedication to the rights-based approach to development – a methodology entrenched in the principles and values of human rights such as equality, accountability, transparency and participation – with later influence from the territorial approach to local development and the resilience-based approach.

CEOSS first instituted an approach of partnership in the 1960s – a tradition that continues to this day, albeit with heavy modification. As part of this tactic, CEOSS routinely designated teams of young program coordinators to spend five days a week in target communities to not only engage with local residents but also provide direct services. These services included social welfare supports, educational/training classes, development programming for rural women, health care and family planning programming, and economic support related to farming and livestock and poultry breeding. These efforts evolved over the subsequent years to include additional areas of focus such as ecological preservation, housing and shelter supports, small-scale economic community development, and other developmental plans. As the agency expanded its services from its initial state as a local literacy program, its geographic reach also increased. All segments of society within the governorates of Cairo, Giza, and Minya were targeted for newly developed services, with no discrimination on the basis of age, gender, or professed religion.

CEOSS began to shift away from providing direct services and toward contemporary community development in the 1980s. This was an important turning point for the agency that set it on the path it continues to follow today.

New emphases were placed on promoting greater self-reliance within target communities, with a focus on increasing the capacity of partners at the local level to define their own community's problems, prioritize issues, and influence the effort to find solutions. By the 1990s, CEOSS's approach to programming had matured: holistic community development, the empowerment of local leadership, and institutional capacity development became central to all of the agency's sustained local programming efforts. In due time, the developmental endeavors of CEOSS began to impact more than two and a half million Egyptian citizens – urban, rural, and semi-urban – on an annual basis.

The strategies of action, as well as the developmental approach pursued over the past years in support of CEOSS's development agenda, have, as outlined below, changed distinctly over time.[1] In the early stages of developmental action, CEOSS put into practice the following two strategies for community development:

1. *The Partnership Approach to Community Development*: This approach traditionally involves six to ten years of extensive and large-scale effort with a focus on providing services and community organization through the creation of resident-led task forces assigned to the targeted communities.

2. *The Follow-Up and Self-Reliant Development Model*: Implementation of this model requires at least five years. This method involves a phase-over plan and an exit strategy, which mandates that the responsibilities associated with the delivery and management of program interventions be handed over to the local leaders by the project team at the end of the project's timeline.

Whether at the stage of participatory community development, follow-up, or self-reliant development, CEOSS has routinely delivered a holistic support program meant to address the problems afflicting the target community within the contexts of health, education, and economy. The standard community development program is comprised of a suite of pre-designed activities and services (such as preventive health-care services and micro-credit loans) a range of technical interventions (i.e., literacy teacher training courses delivered by a team of specialists), and a sequence of interventions around community organization, such as training regarding leadership development as offered by the community development teams. These efforts were reinforced by a series of community-based initiatives specifically tailored to accommodate local

---

1. As indicated in Van Groen and Cramp, "Impact Study."

needs. The community development program was committed to empowering all segments of community to take part in the effort, including Muslim and Christian populations of all sects and denominations.

Customarily, CEOSS-supported programmatic interventions had a traditional focus on outreach and awareness-raising. This type of effort did not only occur within the confines of literacy classes but was also a feature within other programs such as home economics, health and hygiene practices, and training related to agricultural production, animal husbandry/livestock production, and the management of small businesses. This focus reflected the agency's firm belief that social and economic change must be preceded by, or coupled with, an enhancement of the community's general awareness and access to information.

Another important factor in the earlier efforts of CEOSS was local volunteering, mirroring a core principle adopted by CEOSS: the active engagement of individuals in carrying out the interventions that are directly beneficial to their communities. Consequently, one of the common features present across community development actions supported by CEOSS was the promotion of synergy and coordination with grassroots intermediaries, whether in the form of local community committees or existing community-based organizations. This approach was accompanied by the delivery of targeted services through a qualified pool of volunteers (typically dubbed "volunteer leaders"). After the formation of close and robust relationships over a considerable number of years, CEOSS would carry out an exit strategy based on an assumption that the community had developed the capacity required to deliver upon their own goals and services independently.

By 2000, CEOSS moved away from the partnership, follow-up, and self-reliant development models and instead moved toward institutional support efforts and capacity-building programming for community-based organizations (CBOs). These efforts were, naturally, consistent with the agency's new focus upon the capacity-building approach to development. On this basis, CEOSS set out to foster partnerships with developmental intermediaries: civil society organizations (including non-government associations), religious and faith-based organizations, and locally based committees. Prior to this shift, CEOSS had directly delivered services related to its various locally based development programs.

Integration of a Rights-Based Approach to Development

In 2005, CEOSS's development sector put into practice the rights-based approach to development, which involved the following key intervention areas:

1. Increasing representation of disenfranchised and underprivileged populations in government and public agencies and systems (i.e. inclusion).

2. Empowering and enabling disenfranchised/excluded populations to organize themselves, become better acquainted with their rights, and build their capacity to obtain and practice their rights.

3. Engaging in advocacy and lobbying campaigns aimed to facilitate demands and requests for procedural and policy changes in favor of the rights of people who live in poverty.

It is against the backdrop of this development agenda that CEOSS pursued the fight against poverty, striving to improve the quality of life of socially disadvantaged populations most susceptible to poverty, and promote human dignity without discrimination on the grounds of sex, creed, faith, or color.

CEOSS put into practice the rights-based development approach in order to address various areas of concern that have a bearing on development. This task was undertaken in a spirit of partnership and complementarity alongside civil society organizations, competent governmental agencies, research institutions ("think tanks"), academic figures at national universities, figures associated with major media platforms, the private business community, the country's various clerical institutions, and other socially influential entities. These partnerships have delivered a range of programs and interventions, including the following:

- Programs that focus on countering the phenomena of Egyptian child labor, as well as sheltering, rehabilitating, and reintegrating street children into society. Additional focus is placed on enhancing access to education and health rights and on addressing causes of poverty and deprivation.
- Programs that focus on empowerment, integration, and inclusion of persons with disabilities as full members of society, while facilitating their access to public services so that they can enjoy the right to live in dignity in their communities and be fully integrated in society.
- Programs that focus on coordinating national-level efforts to promote greater interest in the issues of persons with disabilities,

while promoting the national movement on accessibility and accommodation.
- Programs that focus on the eradication of illiteracy, conducted in support of those who lack access to formal education and with special consideration given to girls and women.
- Programs that work toward accommodating and supporting those vulnerable groups suffering from a loss of vision/vision impairment. These programs specifically target children experiencing blindness and/or ophthalmic diseases while living among socially disadvantaged/poverty-stricken populations.
- Programs specifically designed to enhance economic empowerment and access to employment, particularly among young people, and increase their employability through vocational training and/or direct vocational recruitment.
- Programs aimed at boosting smallholders' incomes, increasing their productivity, and linking them with more profitable markets (domestic or international) while promoting greater interest in the issues of food security, "bridging the food gap," and enhancing smallholders' contribution to local agricultural development.
- Programs aimed at addressing issues related to housing and shelter, conducted in favor of populations that live in poverty, through structural renovation or dwelling reconstruction.
- Programs focused on civic education, conducted to better promote the concepts of citizenship, tolerance, and mutual acceptance among children and youth.
- Programs centered around capacity building for institutions, with a specific goal of developing the capacity of civil society organizations at the grassroots level. The development of local service cadres (ideally composed of young people) will thus enable those involved to participate actively in building and developing their communities, promote a culture of collective action, enhance community peace-building, and spread the values of tolerance and mutual acceptance.

Additionally, CEOSS dedicated significant resources and efforts toward the development of programming that focused on collaboration with state institutions in order to promote new sustainable and equitable developmental techniques. These approaches included:
- *The Territorial Approach to Rural Development*: Alongside the rights-based approach to Development, CEOSS introduced the

territorial approach to local development in 2011 to better serve underprivileged populations in non-urban Egyptian locales.
- *The Resilience-Based Development Approach*: As part of its development agenda, CEOSS espouses the theory of change (ToC) model. This planning methodology explains the process of change by outlining causal linkages related to the goals of an initiative. The identified changes are then mapped as the "outcomes pathway," showing each outcome in logical relation to other potential outcomes. The links between outcomes are explained via the rationale of why one outcome is thought to be a prerequisite for another, eventually showing how all these outcomes contribute to the achievement of the main goal of change (i.e., building the resiliency of individuals, groups, institutions, and communities to better cope with current and prospective changes while enabling them to effectively assist their communities/constituencies in attaining sustainable goals within an equitable and inclusive framework).

Therefore, CEOSS works closely with grassroots civil society organizations (CSOs), including community-based organizations (CBOs), farmers' cooperative societies, organizations of persons with disabilities, and democratically elected local committees.

The development agenda – as driven by social strengths (that is, development aiming at creating a strong society that has the ability to sustain itself) and the resilience-based development approach – is structured around three major mainstays, as follows:

1. Adaptive capacity development to build resilience at the local level, including the ability to cope, the ability to adapt, and the ability to transform – all, potentially, in the midst of crisis. Efforts are also taken to operationalize/formalize social protection schemes using centrally and locally based incubators and mentoring/coaching models.

2. Poverty reduction by means of empowering local populations that are socially disadvantaged, or populations that otherwise live in poverty, by helping them draft their own plans of change. These plans are arranged using a set of local monitoring and follow-up tools and mechanisms focused around the principles of access to basic rights and services, equal opportunity, equitable sharing of resources, and decent living conditions (as derived from the rights-based approach to development).

3. Promotion of gender balance and equality through efforts to eliminate all forms of discrimination and violence against women. Additionally, efforts are taken to empower women to gain access to newly available resources and opportunities (as derived from CEOSS's "gender mainstreaming" strategy).

The Incubatory Model in Practice

CEOSS utilizes the incubatory model in its developmental work. In order to better promote social resilience, the agency prioritizes work with grassroots civil society organizations and pools of local mentors and coaches. This two-tier model involves a centrally based incubator (hosted at CEOSS headquarters in Cairo) as well as branch incubators within individual target governorates. The centrally based incubator is entrusted with the responsibility to develop plans and methods with a focus on key areas of adaptive capacity development and resilience-building, mentoring and coaching, and the development and delivery of curricular materials and training modules. In addition, the centrally based incubator is responsible for selection and recruitment of consultants and subject matter experts to deliver the targeted training modules. This centrally based incubator trains selected civil society organizations and locally elected committees (ECs) in all stages of project implementation, with a special focus on the social strengths and resilience approach. Through this model, CEOSS works to promote models of funds management, locally driven and resilience-based initiatives, collaboration with sub-national civil society organizations (i.e. at the governorate level), the development of locally based incubators, and consistent engagement with pools of competent mentors and coaches.

The selected pool of mentors and coaches receive extensive and thematic training in the civil society development model, the social strengths and resilience approach (including coping with crises, societal transformation, and social protection strategies), the rights-based approach, locally based monitoring tools, local resource mobilization, advocacy, and techniques by which to monitor change on the local level. These steps are followed by the delivery of the second tier of capacity development interventions – in this case, direct efforts targeting civil society organizations after their selection and institutional capacity assessment. Based on the necessary training modules identified as beneficial for each targeted civil society organization, mentors and coaches are assigned to deliver training and provide close follow-up support to them throughout all stages of capacity building. Additional supports include the selection, design, and delivery of locally driven initiatives and the management of sub-grant funds against the backdrop of the social resilience model.

The incubatory model enables both primary groups – namely, the mentors and coaches as well as the civil society organizations – to experience an insightful, stimulating learning process that incorporates hands-on educational opportunities and training of trainers (ToT) experiences. Under this model, the local mentors/coaches and civil society organizations are afforded an opportunity to practice new skills, sharpen existing skills, and refine existing locally driven initiatives. Upon completion of this capacity development program, the lead participating organization at the sub-national level will be eligible to graduate from the central incubatory program: by the standards of this model, the organization will have been determined as competent to manage the adaptive capacity development and resilience building models in support of grassroots organizations. This final stage marks the climax of the capacity development model, as the lead organizations successfully support the delivery of locally driven initiatives and help achieve their envisaged plans in a decentralized fashion.

At a later time, one lead organization at the sub-national (governorate) level is identified and selected to host the locally based incubator, and assumes responsibility to deliver training modules to grass-roots organizations in selected topics of adaptive capacity development based on the social strengths and resilience-building model. The local incubators, in turn, assumes responsibility for training targeted grassroots civil society organizations in the process of selecting, designing and delivering locally driven, resilience-based initiatives (from a cross section of prioritized sectors of society including health, disability, at-risk children, and local economic development).

In its current state, CEOSS represents an evolved (and evolving) organization: from a decidedly local effort, the agency has unfurled into a multi-faceted organization with dozens of simultaneous efforts pursued both by its veteran staff, reliable partners,[2] and numerous volunteers. The entity's efforts continue to represent work in a number of essential fields: health care, education, economic prosperity, environmentally focused development, and the promotion of dialogue are top priorities for the organization, which has shown a capacity for working from the "ground up" to support local populations through customized services and the eventual goal of self-sufficiency. Working in approximately 184 communities across the country, CEOSS has the privilege

---

2. Including over 1,500 expert consultants and targeted field specialists, as well as individuals representing Egyptian and international research organizations.

to serve approximately three million Egyptians each year, ranging from rural villages to informal urban environments and beyond.

CEOSS Example Initiatives

The fifteen initiatives introduced in this section (ten of which are sub-initiatives that fall under the larger category of CEOSS's coexistence initiative, spearheaded by the Forum for Intercultural Dialogue) are provided as examples. They are not meant to be followed exactly – rather, they should be utilized as models of change on different scales. It does not matter how closely they are emulated or on what scale they are utilized; rather, it is significant to note their potential and effective utility by religiously motivated social service organizations.

1. Protection and Safeguarding of At-Risk Children (Child Laborers and Street Children)

CEOSS gives special consideration to the protection and safeguarding of vulnerable groups of children – particularly child laborers, homeless children, and their families. These populations typically live in socially disadvantaged and impoverished rural and urban areas. In response to their plight, CEOSS has pledged to enhance their living conditions and improve their quality of life. In this context, the developmental efforts exerted by CEOSS are geared toward socially disadvantaged or otherwise destitute children, as well as child laborers who are forced to enter into the labor market due to particularly challenging social and economic conditions. These conditions include a growing opinion among some employers, particularly within labor-intensive crafts, enterprises, and production businesses, that child labor is an opportunity to offer lower pay for productive work while also evading an employer's traditional legal commitments to their workers. In addition, poverty-stricken children are more likely to accept engagement with work under arduous circumstances. With little social leverage, these populations have little choice but to work for low wages during difficult economic times.

For these reasons, CEOSS began to demonstrate interest in the well-being of these vulnerable groups of children as early as the 1990s – and an interest which has continued until the present day. CEOSS, as part of its development agenda, targets child laborers in order to prevent younger children (six to eight years old) from engaging in the labor market. Efforts are taken to help enroll these younger children in formal education, and additional measures are taken to prevent children from dropping out of school after their initial enrollment. Targeted programming is also aimed at older children who are forced, due to their life circumstances, to enter into the labor market. CEOSS has engaged in advocacy in order to protect and safeguard these populations, and efforts have been taken to prevent them from working in hazardous or unsafe environments that can compromise the quality of their life or otherwise interfere with their well-being.

According to the findings of a social assessment survey conducted by CEOSS, the matters that contribute to the phenomena of homeless children ("street children") in Egypt are quite varied. Some key reasons include precarious or unstable family circumstances – the death or incarceration of the family breadwinner, the divorce of a child's parents (thus adding significant stress to the children of those parents), and student absenteeism or "dropping out" of school as a result of school-based violence, unaffordable school expenses, or difficulties engaging with the learning process.

These factors may cause the interruption or discontinuation of a child's education, causing them to become more dependent on the street for their survival – whether as a place to live, a place to work, or a place to find support. It is also worth noting that, if they exist in poverty and abysmal economic conditions, poor families may begin to depend on their children to help relieve the family's sustained financial strain and household expenses. This situation disproportionately affects girls, placing them at increased risk of violence and cruel treatment as they seek work as housemaids and domestic workers. As a result, these children opt to depend on the street for survival. In order to cope with stress, trauma, or everyday troubles, some impacted children begin to use drugs and illegal substances: some children engage in glue-sniffing, for example, as a means by which to avoid feeling physical sensations such as hunger or pain.

In addition, a significant number of these substance-using street children are involved in perpetrating criminal acts in their fight to survive and afford their day-to-day illicit expenses. Without parental protection and guidance, children on the street are vulnerable to many forms of physical, emotional, and sexual abuse. This is compounded by the lack of identity documentation such as birth certificates and identification papers, which are necessary to access basic services such as health insurance and social security coverage; additionally, these populations struggle to safeguard their legal rights without such essential paperwork. This further aggravates an already dangerous situation, as it can lead to an increased denial of the rights of these children as they face greater challenges in simply accessing those rights. This population of children continues to grapple with a sense of perennial fear and anxiety that pushes them away from engagement with mainstream society.

Starting in 2000, CEOSS began to engage with these populations of children. The agency concluded that this initiative was an essential use of time and resources, despite the myriad practical difficulties in working consistently with street children. These efforts were conducted in partnership with other relevant local stakeholders also in pursuit of the children's best interests. By delivering a gamut of development interventions, many opportunities were created to assist with the rehabilitation of these children and to enable them to reclaim their childhood. These efforts included meaningful attempts to return the children to their families, in addition to providing continuous economic, social, and emotional support for those families. With such resources, communities providing economic, social, and emotional support for the families could offer a safe haven and create a secure environment for less fortunate and more vulnerable children. In the same context, or at residential facilities. In other cases, financial and technical/vocational assistance and training were offered to the children in order to increase their economic level of self-reliance. Similarly, efforts were made to teach illiterate children to read and write in conjunction with efforts to reintegrate them into the educational system. Social interventions were also carried out within the wider society to promote the principles of acceptance, inclusiveness, and solidarity among various community groups to create a culture that is more open and receptive to the potential reintegration of this population of children. In doing so, there is some hope that these populations may not continue to experience rejection and ostracism at the hands of their communities and their families.

This multipronged effort demonstrates the commitment of CEOSS to design and deliver interventions deeply entrenched in the agency's rights-based development approach, underpinned by the values and principles of community participation. This is supplemented by partnership and engagement with all stakeholder groups to better assist target communities, with whom, through whom, and for whom we work, in achieving a decent quality of life – in this case, a life of dignity for at-risk children.

CEOSS has been able to successfully promote and reinforce the economic, health, educational, and social rights of at-risk children by means of the following:

- Delivery of a suite of interventions geared toward shielding and safeguarding at-risk children, such as the coordination of vocational/

transformation training (with focus on job change/career transition to facilitate placement of children in less hazardous occupations), along with redeployment and apprenticeship programs.
- Supply of occupational health and safety logistics and equipment to a large number of manufacturing facilities and workshops to better ensure improved and increased access to safe and secure working environments for the advantage of working children. In addition, manufacturers and owners of businesses and workshop facilities who employ large numbers of at-risk children were targeted for an effort to help them develop a common understanding of the fundamental principles and basic rights of children, as well as the importance of ensuring safe and secure working environments (in alignment with the key principles and legal requirements of occupational health and safety).
- Increased access to adequate financial supports for the benefit of low-income families to enable them to continue to send their children to school. In addition, a series of outreach and awareness-raising activities were carried out targeting child laborers and their families as well as homeless children. Proceeding from a rights-based approach, creative learning classes were delivered with a focus on arts education and technological skills development. These initiatives were conducted in partnership with specialist organizations that encouraged at-risk children to develop and express themselves through theater, arts, and comprehensive computer skills. For instance, a group of talented homeless children have been brought together and trained to deliver a theater performance entitled "The Green Light" at the Egyptian Opera House's El-Hanager Arts Centre (as sponsored by, and coordinated alongside, the Ministry of Culture). Many artists, producers, and scriptwriters were motivated to help foster the children's natural innovative talents, as well as nourish the creative vigor of this group, to better enable them to express their thoughts and legal rights through art. This event attracted a large turnout from children, families, and other interested parties, along with a group of young performing artists and media practitioners.
- Development and delivery of information and communications materials to raise awareness with the community at large. For example, leisure and recreational activities – such as social gatherings, outings, camps, and contests – were organized for community members. An

economic empowerment program was designed, targeting a number of women who have at-risk children, to effectively facilitate their access to financial and vocational training. Referral mechanisms to public service providers were put in place to provide a large number of child laborers and homeless children access to education, health care, social welfare, and sports (collaboratively conducted alongside government and non-government organizations).

- Special emphasis is being placed on eliminating the worst forms of agricultural labor through providing access to alternate educational opportunities in community schools. This specifically targets child laborers employed in the agricultural sector to enable them to keep up with their peers in basic formal education, thereby impacting the life of children and their families in an effective fashion.

In general, child laborers and their families – as well as homeless children – lack awareness of their legally enshrined rights and the means by which they can obtain or express such rights. This compounds the tragedy of this group of children, leads to intensification of their hardship, serves to aggravate their suffering, and often leads to violations of their fundamental rights. Therefore, by institutionalizing and popularizing the rights-based approach to development, citizens are introduced and oriented to their rights and obligations. Targeted groups of children are organized into locally elected committees (ECs), which serve as an avenue by which a range of interventions intended to benefit at-risk children can be carried out. At-risk children can practice the principles and modalities of democracy by choosing their own local representatives and are assisted in forming democratically elected committees. These locally elected committees serve as a primary platform from which these children can express themselves, have their voices heard, and advocate for access to their rights – all with the support of various stakeholders and access to supportive services. In addition, monitoring task forces are formed from this group of children to help with the regular identification of the most significant challenges and problems they face.

Additionally, an information task force composed of the same target population has been formed to act as a conduit of communication between media figures and these disadvantaged children. This effort was enacted to support the building up of the children's capacities within the fields of media and information, and some children are given the opportunity to function as youth associate reporters. Furthermore, interfacing meetings were organized by the children's democratically elected committees at the local levels to hold concerned authorities accountable for their actions and choices.

Dedicated lobbying and advocacy mechanisms are central to CEOSS's efforts in this field to ensure that the targeted groups of children have access to their own rights, while holding duty bearers accountable to fulfill their commitments and obligations toward children. CEOSS also underscores these efforts with a call for strengthening the capacities of government and non-government institutions to engage proactively with this matter, through the provision of empowerment and capacity-development interventions focused on network-building. In addition, efforts are made by CEOSS to ensure consolidation of initiatives and actions regarding policy review and legal framework changes to matters such as child labor. Community monitoring, accountability modalities, and continuous engagement with figures engaged in local governance allow for CEOSS to not only stay informed but better inform its target populations and partner organizations of potential new legal challenges or successes in regard to these efforts.

For example, an advocacy campaign was launched with an aim to enforce Article No. 24 of Egypt's Child Law, which ensures respect for the health rights of all children. A locally elected committee subsequently facilitated a process by which to secure the issuance of a resolution mandating the assignment of a duty physician at a health center in the El-Ḥerafeen area of Cairo's Al-Salam City. This initiative was supported by a CEOSS-affiliated non-governmental partner organization in a local community. A toll-free hotline for complaints and reports about the quality of offered medical services was founded, allowing professionals violating Article No. 24 to be reported. This landmark success occurred as a result of ongoing efforts that included face-to-face meetings with public officials and relevant authorities – sessions held in order to hold such figures directly accountable for their actions and decisions, as well as to allow the impacted children to air their grievances and demand their rights to health services.

One of the agency's most important community partners during these advocacy and lobbying efforts is the media – a societal mechanism which is responsible for disseminating information about the difficulties faced by at-risk children. The media has proven able to assist with promoting the rights of marginalized populations, creating platforms for vulnerable populations to shed light upon the hardships they face, and building bridges between various stakeholder groups and rights holders.

2. Fight Against Blindness – Loss of Vision and Preservation of Sight

CEOSS affords special attention to poor and socially disadvantaged populations that are more vulnerable to ophthalmic diseases and the loss/impairment of vision, particularly children, youth, and senior citizens across the least-privileged urban, semi-urban, and rural areas.

Estimates from the World Health Organization (WHO) indicate that 80 percent of the causes of visual impairment, if diagnosed and treated in a timely manner, can be prevented or cured.[3] The 2009 findings of the WHO's rapid assessment of avoidable blindness (RAAB) revealed that Egypt is among the countries most vulnerable to issues related to the loss or impairment of vision. The number of persons without functional vision in Egypt has been estimated at nearly one million, while there exist approximately three million Egyptians who suffer from visual impairments. According to this same study, 60 percent of those who are visually impaired are diagnosed with cataracts (i.e. clouding of the lens of the eye) – an easily alleviated affliction that can contribute to more serious issues if not treated. If measures such as medical screenings and diagnostic testing services for ophthalmic diseases/disorders are undertaken on a large scale, and in conjunction with the public health system, Egypt will be able to reduce the incidences of vision loss, contributing not only to the quality of life of afflicted individuals but also to their rates of societal participation and vocational productivity. If paired with pre-operative medical testing and widely available cataract surgical procedures, the rates of such an endeavor's success will increase exponentially.

CEOSS's ophthalmological and eye health development agenda is, at the local level, focused on reduction of the root causes of treatable/avoidable blindness among poor populations – those at a greater risk of loss/impairment of vision – in order to assist in breaking the cycle of poverty and increasing the productivity of the afflicted individuals. These initiatives are undertaken alongside efforts to strengthen the national systems related to eye health care and further enable Egyptian health systems and institutions to become more inclusive in their consideration of this issue.

In this context, CEOSS carries out a series of development interventions, including prompt and urgent interventions focused on protection from and treatment of avoidable blindness and various types of ophthalmic diseases and disorders. Such interventions include provision of medical screening and diagnostic testing services through CEOSS-supported mobile health units,

---

3. WHO, "Blindness and Vision Impairment," accessed 25 November 2020, https://www.who.int/news-room/fact-sheets/detail/blindness-and-visual-impairment.

entities that are supplied with the state-of-the-art equipment and staffed with a specialized team of health/nursing professionals. These teams are able to reach out to those residents of small hamlets and villages in rural, semi-urban, and urban areas who are most in need of immediate assistance. By making these degrees of expertise accessible, comprehensive ophthalmic diagnostic and therapeutic services are provided to thousands of citizens annually with particular focuses on children and women. Such services include offering pharmaceutical treatment solutions, a range of vision correction services such as prescription spectacles, and surgical procedures to treat eye cataracts, as coordinated through a referral system to Horus Eye Hospital (operated by CEOSS in Minya Governorate) and other partner hospitals that offer services of the same nature.

In addition, CEOSS puts into practice a suite of measures to strengthen and promote the operationalization and institutionalization of national policies and plans concerned with matters of universal eye health and ophthalmology. Efforts are made by CEOSS to contribute to revisions and amendments of national plans and polices concerned with prevention of avoidable visual impairment and ophthalmic diseases/disorders, in addition to efforts made to ensure that citizens have the right to exercise their voices on the subject of their own health rights. Health-care institutions and the national health-care systems have been targeted for interventions that call for the mainstreaming of ocular health-care services, the further development of health-care infrastructure, the dissemination of modern medical equipment, and increased access to medical facilities. In collaboration with subject matter experts, CEOSS has developed capacity-building programs focused on the delivery of substantive information related to ocular health and ophthalmic diseases/disorders; these capacity building programs are held concurrently with capacity-development sessions for health professionals meant to enhance the manner in which they engage with the public. Furthermore, efforts are made to develop and capitalize on democratic capacity at the local level, an effort undertaken to enable affected populations to advocate for policy amendments and modified regulatory procedures at the local level.

Secondary efforts are also taken to reinforce all the aforementioned initiatives in order to guarantee a sustained effort regarding eye health care. Mechanisms of referral to health-care institutions have been reviewed and redeveloped in order to facilitate access to medical screening and diagnostic services at primary health-care institutions, with the possibility of referring cases that require more thorough medical examination or surgical procedures to specialist ophthalmological hospitals. Additionally, efforts are ongoing to raise community awareness about the systems and policies that have been put in place; this step is being taken in order promote public scrutiny and attention to these matters, and continues today with collaboration from governmental agencies and relevant national health-care commissions. Ideally, this will enable the institutionalization of a more inclusive and sustainable health system in Egypt.

Drawing from the tenets of the rights-based approach to development, orientation meetings have been coordinated in order to raise community awareness of common ocular problems and disorders that act as the main causes of blindness. These sessions serve as an opportunity to mobilize action at the local level and create a strong constituency in support of these concerns, which are problems that overtly impact less-fortunate populations more vulnerable to ophthalmic diseases and blindness. Efforts are also made to ensure adequate representation of the rights holders in electoral constituencies and locally elected committees, the main platforms from which the demands of rights holders are heard. These representative committees are democratically elected from local communities in order to elevate the voices of these same rights holders, and in this context, many concerns have been related regarding the state of ocular health and eye care in Egypt. Among the main tasks assumed by the locally elected committees are the coordination of public discussions related to the subjects of ocular health and eye care, the tracking of unmet rights and forgone services in the local medical field, and the status of efforts to mainstream ophthalmology into the primary health-care system. Even more, these committees are empowered and enabled to represent the interests of the rights holders at the national level, as well as to ensure changes to existing systems and that measures and policies concerned with the area of ocular health and care are addressed. Toward this end, advocacy and lobbying campaigns are consistently launched and sustained in conjunction with CEOSS's many partners.

Based on the expressed interest of citizens' organizations that work in this field to address their communities' needs, particular attention is paid to collaboration with community-based partner organizations to build up their institutional, organizational, managerial, and technical capabilities. With such upgrades, these organizations will be better able to advocate on behalf of socially disadvantaged and impoverished populations existing within the target communities. In addition, these groups are supported in the creation of their own policies regarding access to ocular care and eye health services for the aforementioned target populations. Alongside government authorities, community liaisons continue to secure sustained delivery of such services in an accessible, inclusive, and high-quality fashion.

3. Working with Persons with Disabilities

CEOSS has demonstrated an earnest interest in improving the quality of life for Egyptian people with disabilities. CEOSS developed a revolutionary approach to address issues of disability: moving away from the medical, functionalist, and social intervention model, the organization instead began to work under the rights-based approach to development. Through this model, CEOSS treats issues related to those with disabilities as a top priority. The respectful treatment of persons with disabilities – human beings, inherently deserving the same access to life and society as people without disabilities – is a matter of human rights. Yet, instead of receiving these rights, these human beings are subject to discrimination, stigmatization, and social exclusion. Popularly, a "disability" is understood to be a disorder or deficiency in the human capacity to perform his or her normal life activities or functions, or execute a task or action.[4] In reality, disability is a dynamic confluence of multiple personality factors, represented in a certain dysfunction, a lack of competency, or difficulties stemming from environmental factors (such as structural barriers or hurdles). According to the Convention on the Rights of Persons with Disabilities, "disability" is an evolving, dynamic, and non-static concept that varies depending on the framework and context in which it is addressed. Based on this framework, the empowerment of persons with disabilities – which include efforts to enhance the quality of their living conditions and promote their integration in society and equal and fair access to rights and services – is one of the most significant CEOSS-supported developmental programs.

CEOSS supports this program via a twin-track approach: (1) promotion of both the empowerment of disabled persons and (2) a separate effort to enhance national accessibility and cultivate a culture more inclusive of persons with disabilities.

Track 1

The first track entails the empowerment of persons with disabilities such as those related to mobility, hearing, sight, and mental health. Under this track, efforts are made to improve their quality of life and to encourage their

---

4. CDC, "Disability and Health Overview," accessed 25 Nov 2020, https://www.cdc.gov/ncbddd/disabilityandhealth/disability.html.

integration in society; at the same time, steps are taken to reduce or eliminate environmental and cultural barriers that negatively impact the well-being of persons with disabilities, including cultural misconceptions, conceptual frameworks inherited from attitudes prevalent in society, and all forms of discrimination and restrictions that hamper their access to their own rights. Similar efforts are made to enhance the capacity of those service providers working with persons with disabilities, as well as the capacity of those persons with disabilities themselves. Additionally, efforts are made to better inform and educate their family members and caregivers.

In the spirit of empowerment and in order to better help persons with disabilities, CEOSS offers specialized services and support programs for persons with disabilities at the local level. CEOSS has established several community-based rehabilitation facilities to provide programming to both persons with disabilities and their families, allowing for the local implementation of services including early intervention programs, medical rehabilitation, motor skills training and rehabilitative physiotherapy, academic and vocational rehabilitation, and therapeutic speech services. As part of these programs, training is provided to local personnel from the targeted communities to enable them to provide rehabilitation programs using context-appropriate and inclusive methods. In addition, CEOSS provides access to accommodative mobility aids, prosthetic devices, and assistive services to persons with disabilities in need of material supports. In a first for the greater Arab region, CEOSS has also implemented a program that promotes the societal participation of persons with mild and moderate intellectual disabilities – not as beneficiaries but rather as key actors in the coordination and management of inclusive development models within local communities.

Over the years, CEOSS has accumulated a range of on-the-ground experiences relevant to the coordination of community groups working toward promoting the rights and service access of persons with disabilities. This has been recognized as an important mechanism in implementing the rights-based approach to development, as well as promoting engagement and participation of persons with disabilities as rights holders and key figures in local development. The primary purpose of these actions is to create and sustain a locally driven and grassroots-based democratic movement that involves persons with disabilities at the community level, allowing those already involved in this effort to more competently defend and advocate for the rights of persons with disabilities.

Over the past ten years, CEOSS has supported a process of community organization targeting more than twenty thousand people to form fifty locally elected committees – entities that are broadly representative of the rights and interests of persons with disabilities – in addition to continuing to support groups of persons with disabilities who are members of the locally elected committees. CEOSS works to support and empower them to establish and register a number of disabled persons organizations (DPOs), which will work toward the specific local benefit of affected persons in different communities. CEOSS also presented a series of capacity-building training sessions for activists, advocates, and persons with disabilities to educate and inform them on the matter of building community-based groups and organizations to further support this effort. These steps mobilized a pool of activists who are currently involved in establishing a strong, locally driven movement in support of persons with disabilities.

On the national level, CEOSS has explored a number of avenues for partnering, networking, and working closely with associations and groups of persons with disabilities across Egypt. This history has led to the establishment of a partnership of associations for the disabled persons of Egypt. This organization, the Egyptian Forum for Persons with Disabilities, brings together a number of associations of persons with disabilities, as well as locally elected committees (representing persons with disabilities) from twenty-three Egyptian governorates, including border governorates.

The Egyptian Forum for Persons with Disabilities seeks to promote participation of persons with disabilities via efforts to positively influence the formulation of public policies and help relay the voices of persons of disabilities to a greater audience. Efforts were made by the Egyptian Forum for Persons with Disabilities to share in drafting a proposal for legislation regarding the matter of disabled persons for incorporation into the Egyptian Constitution of 2014, specifically Article No. 20. In addition, the forum generated expert proposals to assist with the improvement and amendment of the Egyptian law on people with disabilities in 2017. Members of the Egyptian Forum for Persons with Disabilities, along with CEOSS representatives, were invited to sit in meetings held in the Egyptian Parliament during the discussion process of the draft law.

Track 2

As part of the second track of CEOSS's Accessibility and Creation of Inclusive Environments Initiative, CEOSS actively embraces the notion that "disability is a social construct." The idea argues that disability is a perception that is based mainly on the extent to which individuals are integrated or isolated within a society. CEOSS believes that efforts directed toward addressing issues of disability require a change in mindsets on a grand scale, as well as the mobilization of social responsibility, in order to create a welcoming, barrier-free environment that can further promote the active involvement of persons with disabilities in all spheres of life.

Against this background, CEOSS established a factory called Iraḍa (literally translated as "the will") centered on the production of wheelchairs, assistive devices for people with motor disabilities, and prosthetic limbs for amputees. Additionally, the agency formed a specialized manufacturing unit to draft designs and proposals for environmental accessibility adaptations and structural changes within some public and private institutions, as well as suggestions for house layout configurations that are more accessible for persons with disabilities. The factory is staffed with a team of workers with disabilities who have been trained to work productively in accessible environments, as well as a team of technical staff specializing in the implementation of environmental assessments, the development of architectural designs that are "disability friendly," and technical support for outside institutions and individuals. This factory is supported by an outreach team that is responsible for raising community awareness around the issue of disability in an effort to change popular perceptions and stereotypical notions about disabled persons, as well as to pursue and foster partnerships with private, public, and community-based actors. CEOSS also gives due attention to the promotion of accessibility measures and other supportive policies as related to the social responsibilities of private entities and corporations. CEOSS seeks to build customized, replicable, and scalable learning models that are well-suited for creating change within the Egyptian environment.

In 2017, CEOSS recruited an international expert from India to produce a toolkit to allow for assessment of the public service availability, query response time, and levels of societal access – as well as a review of delivered services – for Egyptian persons with disabilities. This internationally recognized assessment aid was used to create a disability-inclusive auditing system: a necessary tool in identifying issues with accessibility and accommodation in public and private construction designs and drafts.

These efforts by CEOSS have not been limited to Egypt. Rather, the agency set out to partner and network with the largest entity in community-based rehabilitation (CBR) in the African continent: the CBR Africa Network, a leading independent and international learning platform that facilitates information-sharing on disability, community-based rehabilitation programming, and inclusive development within Africa and across the world.

CEOSS is an official African regional affiliate of the CBR Global Network – an organization with a membership that comprises several hundred African institutions that operate in the area of disability. The member agencies of this organization work together to utilize their expertise and promote cross-fertilization of experiences, thus facilitating the transfer of CEOSS's field experience in the area of disability to other communities in Africa.

4. Facilitating the Organization of Small Farmers

The primary purpose of CEOSS's supportive agrarian programs is to improve the quality of life for smallholder farmers – those producers who either own or rent up to three feddans of land,[5] and who account for an average of 85 percent of Egypt's farming population. Evidently, this social group engages with the agricultural sector against the backdrop of challenging social and economic conditions that offer low prospects of adequate financial return. Subsequently, few smallholder farmers achieve a decent life replete with social dignity. Goals for improved economic opportunities and quality of life are supported through projects related to rural area development, and the empowerment of smallholders, to better capitalize on their existing resources, potentials, and expertise. Small farmers are supported in transforming their local competence into a competitive advantage that can reap dividends at the social, environmental, and economic levels.

CEOSS seeks to enable groups of farmers, producers, and fishermen to work in groups, clusters or associations, in accordance with democratic and constitutional principles. These assembled groups can practice democracy in choosing their own representatives – figures responsible for speaking before private sector corporations and government authorities to demand access to their community's economic and human rights. Particular issues of concern for this group are targeted by this outreach, and efforts are made to connect this population of producers to more profitable or lucrative markets through systemic application of the rights-based approach to development and the territorial approach to local development, and specific steps are taken to increase the value of the products produced within the target communities.

As mentioned, the agrarian programs are best characterized by the organization of small farming communities into informal, grassroots-styled

---

5. A feddan is a unit of measurement used in Egypt and surrounding countries. In Egypt, 1 feddan equals 4.2 square kilometers.

groups/clusters, with representatives that are democratically elected by the constituents of each community. The decentralized nature of these groups allows for each community to have its rights represented by someone local and accommodates the different traditional and systemic forms of elected governance. These locally based organizations are mandated to aggregate the individual decisions and issues relevant to small farmers into a form of collective action. Through appropriate representation and engagement in farmers' associations, these smallholders are reinforced in their efforts to demand and defend their own rights, achieve their best economic and social interests, and overcome challenges associated with local agriculture (land fragmentation, reduction of yields, and exploitation by middlemen).

Small farmers' organizations are defined and recognized by CEOSS as one of the agency's most vital and consistent applications of the rights-based approach to development. These organizations seek to provide significant and essential supports to small farmers – real support that is capable of amounting for tangible changes in their living conditions. The farmers' associations are voluntary, locally driven organizations that are formed on the principles of domestic fairness and electoral choice; their participants, although possessing a relatively small and fragmented amount of agricultural influence, shift from a role of powerless and invisible individuality into a significant, powerful force at the market level that can exert an influence on policy formulation. The formation of these local organizations follows a progressive and logical approach: a proper pacing is adopted during the process of their formation, complete with a sequencing and calibration process. Through the application of democratic principles and the eventual representation of their constituents through elected committees, the organizations are accessible to – and representative of – all target small farmers, serving them at the community level.

Throughout the stages of assisting with the formation of these democratically elected committees, CEOSS seeks to promote the principles of empowerment, transparency, social justice, and anti-discriminatory action. These efforts have a "trickle-down" effect of influencing other societal groups to consider engagement with electoral politics and democratic practices, thus enriching the representative and participatory capacities of local government. In addition, women are vigorously encouraged to participate at every step of a group's formation as full members in the collective. These democratically elected committees have, to date, shown themselves capable of lending significant support to the work of Egyptian small farmers. Advocacy and lobbying campaigns have been launched by the organizations with an aim to influence solutions to a range of constraints facing their constituents.

One of the examples of these constraints was a trend of insufficient and inadequate access to healthy irrigation water at the tertiary-canal level. These tertiary canals are very important for the irrigation of Egyptian farmlands, and they often serve a large number of rural villages. If a problem affected one portion of a canal, this local problem would quickly become a much larger problem due to the interconnected reliance of many communities on any one canal. Small farmers would be impacted distinctly, as a lack of irrigation would have a severely adverse impact upon the quality and productivity of the already low-yield agricultural lands possessed by small farmers.

The farmers' associations took action, engaging in multi-pronged efforts to respond to such a crisis. Advocacy and lobbying events were held, including face-to-face meetings with relevant government officials to bring to their attention the problems and constraints facing small farmers and their communities. Petitions demanding support and specific measures were presented to these individuals and were also available to the public through media organizations and public information campaigns. As a result of these efforts, the concerned authorities generated a prompt response to solve the problems as defined by the farmers' associations: efforts were made to clear blockages within the canal, including the removal of several tons of waste. As a result, the water once again flowed into the canal system. Additionally, water availability was extended to underserved areas through canal maintenance efforts. The small farmers were thus able to respond to a local problem and benefit from such an effort.

In supporting these organizations, CEOSS places emphasis on the expansion and continuous development of the small farmers' organizational model in order to best ensure that each community is engaged with a form of the model that benefits and represents its constituents. Such democratically elected groups and associations have proved to be successful and locally invigorating. As a result, democratically elected committees have been established at the governorate-level in order to promote social causes – particularly issues of agriculture and their impact on small farmers, as well as advocacy and lobbying campaigns supporting farmers' causes and demanding responsive action from the authorities.

In order to ensure continuity and to achieve a sustainable and successful return on the democratically elected committees representing small farmers at the local and sub-national (governorate) levels, efforts were made to facilitate official government registration of these committees into cooperative societies with a formalized status. These new steps also assisted in the enhancement of the availability of local agricultural services across target communities.

The composition of newly established cooperatives consists of members of elected committees at the governorate-level (i.e., representatives of the elected smallholders' communities). Such cooperatives are run and operated autonomously by elected small farmers, and act to represent the specific and local interests of involved farmers in each governorate.

Such cooperatives offer services to their own members to assist with the cultivation of arable crops and to monitor the implementation of crop schedules that are agreed upon with input from regional government agricultural plans. Furthermore, these cooperatives are responsible for carrying out regular market and soil studies in order to promote the cultivation of crops that are safe for human consumption and free from harmful chemical substances, in consistency with the international parameters of agricultural production. The organizations take part in the organization and regulation of local farmlands on the basis of sound scientific principles, doing so in cooperation with government agencies, local government units, and research centers. In doing so, the farmers' associations ensure the marketing support and commercial viability of the crop yields within the area of operation of each respective cooperative. These cooperatives also seek to espouse social causes and advocacy issues at the governorate-level in favor of farmers, in order to ensure ease of access to services and agricultural technology distributed by local governments – such as essential equipment or modifications, including irrigation water sharing arrangements and high-yield fertilizer – while streamlining bureaucratic procedures.

CEOSS will continue to empower and enable small farmers to exercise democracy as they choose their representation via the democratically elected committees and small farmers' cooperatives. This, in turn, will facilitate the access of small farmers to government institutions in order to maximize the utility of government assets and resources, build their capacity in market analysis, and enable them to engage in successful negotiations regarding private contracts. Farmers will continue to be supported in enhancing the quality of their agricultural products, allowing them to achieve higher levels of productivity and distribute their goods at more competitive prices and within an expanded range of markets. Finally, these locally driven, democratically elected groups of small farmers will continue to serve as a critical community-driven vehicle in promoting gender balance and upholding the important role of women in agricultural activities – a feature that will further boost the average household income and survival ability of those participating in the farmers' associations.

5. Empowering Women and Combating Violence and Prejudicial Practices against Women and Girls

A central priority of CEOSS's developmental agenda has been advancing the status of Egyptian women and issues associated with Egyptian women. Within these efforts, an emphasis is placed on the matter of combating violence against women and girls – a task of special importance due to the popular cultural perception that violence against women and girls is a women's issue. In reality, violence against women and girls is a serious concern to be addressed by all of Egyptian society.

CEOSS works intently on combating violence against Egyptian women and the elimination of practices that are particularly prejudicial and harmful for girls and women, such as female genital mutilation (FGM), early marriage, and a lack of education for girls and women. Since the late 1960s and early 1970s, CEOSS has embarked on a series of awareness-raising campaigns and outreach projects directed at rural communities through household visits and education seminars that call for greater attention to be paid to the health and education of women through adult literacy classes and home economic classes. CEOSS recognized the intense need for women's empowerment, and it began to regularly promote public awareness of all forms of discrimination and abuse (physical and emotional) faced by women and girls in Egypt. These initial steps were followed by a wide-ranging empowerment effort across many of the local communities supported by CEOSS, particularly in rural areas and informal settlements in urban and semi-urban areas. In committing to this issue, CEOSS experienced many successes but also experienced a number of constraints, particularly as they engaged with oppositional community groups. This dichotomy resulted in the creation of the first practical models of engagement with Egyptian villages on this issue. In response to the institution of the engagement models, community members in villages such as Deir Al-Barsha (Mallawi District, Minya Governorate) and Izbat Jaafar (Al-Fashn District, Beni Suef Governorate) pledged to refrain from engaging in the practice of female genital mutilation (FGM). Influential leaders in these two communities signed a document acknowledging their consent to forbid and partner in eliminating the practice of FGM in their local communities.

CEOSS has made a firm and continuous effort to work with Egyptian women to promote improvements related to quality of life and standard of living. Originating from a sense of social responsibility, and acted upon since the agency's inception, CEOSS views efforts to empower women as a critical path toward the continuing advancement of Egyptian society. Promotion of women's quality of life and well-being cannot be reached through only the introduction of anti-violence measures, however. The concrete empowerment of women is key to sustained anti-violence efforts. It is against this backdrop in particular that CEOSS decided to put into effect a number of actionable strategies – including the rights-based approach to development, empowerment and capacity-building campaigns, advocacy, and political lobbying – to work toward this sought progress.

The rights-based approach to development aims to promote justice, equality, and freedom for all women while placing emphasis on the standards, principles, and norms of human rights as essential components for the agency's development programs. This strategy is enacted in tandem with consistent promotion of the fair treatment of women within Egyptian society. CEOSS has delivered a broad spectrum of programs and interventions, including the inclusion of women in elected committees, building women's capacity to articulate and defend their legal rights. In addition, CEOSS has focused on partnering and networking with government authorities – entities considered as societal "duty bearers" – in order to pursue a more concerted approach to empowerment efforts. Several meetings, workshops, and seminars have been organized to review and discuss the policy framework regulating the rights of women in all spheres of life. Statements and clarifications of rights gleaned from these sessions were then disseminated to the public through different media platforms and information outlets (audio-visual media, print media, information and communication materials such as publications and leaflets, and awareness-raising meetings).

Furthermore, CEOSS has sought to enable women to become better acquainted with their own rights across all spheres of life and how to employ best social practices to demand their rights from the persons or authorities responsible for the fulfillment of those rights. Public sessions are regularly held to support women's participation in the process of planning and delivering the development programs offered to them by CEOSS. When accompanied with the involvement of legal professionals and members of parliament, these events also serve as an opportunity to present and review flawed legislation and resolutions that hamper women's access to their own rights. CEOSS has implemented additional advocacy and lobbying programs to discuss the need to institute legal reforms and amend legislation as needed.

Within the framework of women's empowerment and capacity building, CEOSS also employs a supplementary focus on supporting and strengthening elected committees. These groups are representative of the women within target communities, and as such have the ability to amplify women's voices –

especially when women within a target community are demanding access to their rights. CEOSS has made every effort to build the capacity of government and non-government organizations to better perform their democratic mission in a manner that positively impacts Egyptian society in general, and the state of Egyptian women in particular. In this context, CEOSS has coordinated a number of specialist-supported programs aimed at governmental units in regard to the specific needs of target communities. These programs address a range of thematic areas, such as teamwork and collaborative work, and emphasize direct engagement with local community figures, regular communication and outreach, the importance of volunteering and public service, networking and partnership-building, transparency and accountability, advocacy/lobbying, and issues related to human rights. These meetings are organized to facilitate the exchange of experiences among local residents, specifically women, within the same community. Subsequently, these events often act to facilitate the transfer of the experiences of women who have been successfully empowered. In addition, programs have been designed to build the capacity of community partners – both individuals and local agencies – to better orient them to their roles and responsibilities within the field of empowerment. These partners are encouraged to support this mandate via engaging in CEOSS-directed efforts to work toward the full development and empowerment of women.

Advocacy and lobbying also form an important supportive pillar within CEOSS's extensive efforts to support the well-being of Egyptian women. Special emphasis is placed on responding to the underlying causes of women's societal marginalization, the issue of violence against women and girls, and the failure to fulfill their fundamental rights in all spheres of society. Discussion events are held in order to discuss and enact the necessary amendments to legislative and policy frameworks as related to the rights and status of women. In this context, CEOSS has achieved many significant victories: the organization participated in the drafting of a law offering free medical examinations for individuals entering marriage and took part in the review of many laws passed by previous parliaments in order to improve the economic status of women. In addition, CEOSS contributed to a policy document identifying key economic elements to be included in Egypt's new constitution. This document was submitted to the fifty-member constitutional committee and contained a particular focus on women's economic status. CEOSS also called for the institutionalization of several laws and ministerial resolutions that would facilitate political access for citizens, in particular women, to a number of unfulfilled rights that impact a number of fields in which CEOSS works. Some of these related issues included the protection of students considering dropping out of school, access to free education, the inclusion of children under a parent's free health insurance coverage, and a mandate for a 5 percent quota for employing people with disabilities. These steps have been taken in conjunction with an increased emphasis on women's involvement in the efforts made to address these issues: women are organized in semi-formal or parastatal organizations that support the building of their capacities, the raising of their awareness, and the enabling of their abilities to demand their rights.

In addition, women are empowered across other development aspects, including the following:

- *Enhancement of Women's Economic Status.* Vocational training is offered for women in target communities and is made available to girls and women interested in the fields of handicrafts or related industries. Local entities also deliver micro-credit programs to support small businesses and craft enterprises, the organizing of employment fairs at the local and regional levels, assistance with providing women access to employment opportunities through partner networks, and contributions to several legal protocols that guarantee the availability of existing vocational services for women. Some notable partners in establishing these protocols are the Ministry of Manpower, Egyptian academic universities, the private business community, entities within civil society, the Ministry of Youth, and the Egyptian Chamber of Commerce. Furthermore, capacity-building interventions are carried out around important topics such as marketing and branding skills, business management, personalized marketing, and quality accreditation.
- *Improved Quality of Formal and Information Education.* Literacy classes are offered for women who live in poor areas, with special attention paid to female students taking part in basic education programming in order to help them overcome all the obstacles associated with their academic learning. Remedial education programs are also made available and accessible to underachieving students to ensure their retention in education. Opportunities to develop and strengthen technical and cognitive skills are offered specifically to female students, while civic education programs are offered to female students in order to reinforce values of citizenship and societal belonging. Female students are encouraged to join student unions and student parliamentary models so as to enhance the value of democratic participation and assist in the development

of a generation of female students with strong leadership potential. Community participation opportunities are created to allow female students to engage in outreach and contribute to their communities; within those same communities, social dialogue activities are conducted with the participation of beneficiary women, government officials, local figures, and regional decision makers to process matters related to the status of women and their place in Egyptian society.
- *Greater Attention to Women's Health and Emotional Welfare.* Prenatal and antenatal health-care services are offered to pregnant women through regular clinical checkups, and local health-care programs targeting women in the post-reproductive age are carried out. Continued efforts are made to combat FGM practices through mobilizing community resources in response to this practice. To supplement these activities, assistance in obtaining psychological support and legal assistance is provided to women who have been victims of violence or abuse. Informational and communication materials are made publicly available to raise the awareness of women about methods by which they can combat violence; to this end, CEOSS has partnered with Egypt's Human Rights Support Network – an entity that has published a number of books and materials supporting women's access to health, safety, and legal rights. Additionally, CEOSS provides support to governmental agencies to assist them in the delivery of pre-marital medical examinations, family counseling programs, and health counseling programs.

6. Coexistence Initiative: The Forum for Intercultural Dialogue (FID)

As discussed in detail in chapter 3 of this text, the matter of coexistence is of grand importance to Egyptian society. The Forum for Intercultural Dialogue (FID), one of CEOSS's most progressive and expansive endeavors, acts as the agency's contribution to this important effort.

Since its inauguration, CEOSS has been striving to inform a view of Egyptian society that is not limited to perceptions influenced by societal distinctions, class, or expressions of faith. The vision of Egypt promoted by CEOSS is not one in which any group's opinions or needs are prioritized over another – rather, it is an inclusive vision of a diverse nation. Over time, the agency has recognized a distinct need to engage in both internal and external dialogue in order to promote these values.

The FID is a unit focused on the field of culture. Originally part of CEOSS's development sector, the FID started as a pilot forum. Over time and through increased project activity, it was formally titled The Department of Studies and Dialogue and became its own department within CEOSS. Throughout the following years, the FID concept has been put to use in multiple executive and demonstrative frameworks. The forum began by initiating meetings between the leaders of non-governmental organizations in Minya and promoting dialogue between Christian and Islamic religious leaders in CEOSS's target communities. The meetings were attended by a number of Christian religious leaders, scholars representing Egypt's prominent Al-Azhar University, and governmental figures from Egypt's Supreme Council for Islamic Affairs and the Ministry of Endowment. From this effort, a dialogue group was formed of those concerned with public affairs; university professors, religious leaders, media professionals, and social workers readily took part. The group's focus was shifted to discussing potential social efforts and joint planning through community programs, including events held with the Ministry of Endowment. At these sessions, young preachers and priests discussed subjects related to the importance of citizenship, religious coexistence, the promotion of peace, and the essential task of accepting Egyptian diversity.

Since its inception, the FID has continuously sought to support a culture of dialogue, diversity, and acceptance of the "other." In addition, the FID has also sought to contribute to the ideal of establishing a healthy and interactive environment for communication, supporting the principles of democracy and citizenship, and reinforcing community efforts toward collective work. These initiatives have been undertaken in order to promote a culture of coexistence – namely, one that can assist in the fight against religious extremism and cultural isolationism. The FID has also engaged in initiatives related to the promotion of the development of an Egyptian society devoted to the values of citizenship, the principles of human rights, respect for diversity, and a preference for utilizing fair and legal institutional means to resolve disputes. In recent years, the objectives and approaches of the FID – as related to culture, social development, and political shifts – have taken into consideration both current events and potential events that could impact the state of the Egyptian nation. Recent conferences held by the FID pertained to matters such as "Culture and Development in the Face of Fundamentalism," "Partnerships for the Sake of Sustainable Development," and "Egypt Is for All Egyptians."

The FID is keen not to be confined to meeting rooms. Rather, the department is more concerned with direct communication between governmental organizations, civil society organizations (CSOs), and grassroots partners through joint efforts to design and implement community initiatives that target the most culturally vulnerable and marginalized: the poor in general, and women and children specifically. To work toward this goal, the FID has utilized different approaches including art, dialogue sessions, activities oriented toward the exchange of experiences, and training sessions. In addition, the agency makes efforts to activate local partners, governmental organizations, and locally representative committees in their efforts to enact change on a local and tangible level.

In partnership with the different departments of CEOSS, the FID has adopted several integrated development models with the purpose of improving the quality of life of vulnerable and marginalized groups. The FID puts these models to use as it introduces and facilitates positive, long-reaching initiatives to confront the most urgent community issues, with a particular focus on cultural and social issues.

Out of its belief that the Egyptian youth are the future of the nation, the FID has been concerned with culturally empowering this sizeable group. Youth working in academic, informational, and cultural NGOs and CSOs are regularly invited to take part in leadership seminars and events that provide them with coaching/mentorship opportunities and customized tools to assist them in their work.

At the same time, the FID has continued building public diplomacy partnerships and international relations projects. The department has held many international dialogue sessions in cooperation with a number of concerned organizations, both inside and outside of Egypt. This dialogue is not limited to organizational partnerships, however: it has also extended to meetings with a number of officials representing European countries and the United States. Some of the FID's ongoing efforts in this regard are the Arab-Arab Dialogue, the European-Arab Dialogue, the Arab-German Dialogue, and the Arab-American Dialogue. Since the June 30 Revolution, the FID has been contributing to a more accurate image of Egypt for those outside of the country while also bridging more formal diplomatic and cultural gaps.

These projects – and their successes – would not be possible if not achieved in unity between FID and its tireless, supportive partners. Such efforts have come to fruition only through cooperation with Egyptian research centers and universities (such as Al-Azhar University), media and press organizations, governmental entities such as the Ministry of Endowment, and long-time partners of Egypt's church community. Consequently, the FID has focused on strengthening these partnerships while establishing new relationships with organizations including UNESCO, UNDP, and other internationally relevant groups. The FID has continued to cooperate with local community-based development organizations (CBOs) and NGOs to find solutions to problems on the local, regional, and international levels.

Content of FID Issues that Support Coexistence Principles

Over the course of FID's tenure, many efforts have been made to record and assess the discussions held between intellectuals, governmental figures, religious leaders, and other conference participants. From their work, the following conclusions have been agreed upon.

- The FID has reflected upon the issues and concerns expressed by members of Egyptian society in relation to its current events. The FID has utilized dialogue in order to identify Egypt's central issues and to find solutions that contribute toward the building of a modern democratic state. The FID has readily discussed issues relevant to democratic transition, barriers to progress, economic difficulties and the means by which the nation could overcome them, the repercussions of economic reform on social life, the importance of combating poverty, and the necessity of maintaining national cohesion in the face of terrorism.
- The FID has drawn attention to significant and critical problems for all Egyptians, including issues most relevant to youth and women – two groups that have become more active in their efforts to achieve social justice, engage with the media, and work toward democratic initiatives. The FID has processed issues related specifically to Upper Egypt, the potential future of the nation, efforts to combat violence and terrorism, the shift toward an Egyptian democratic transition, and the relationship between Muslims and Christians during this critical phase of Egyptian history.
- The FID has performed a useful public service in assessing and explaining the details of new constitutional articles, highlighting the issue of renewing religious discourse in the current era, the important role of religious leaders in building the future of Egypt, the necessity of an informed public community, and the role of scientific research in development work with a focus on human rights.

- The FID has become concerned with the role of civil society and how it could be modified to better benefit Egyptian society. Due to its belief that no modern democratic country can function without an active and thriving civil society, the FID has made efforts to shed light upon obstacles facing the participants of civil society. Accordingly, in many FID events, particularly workshops, participants identify the role that should be played by the civil society in each issue addressed. Moreover, the FID has also focused on disseminating a culture of volunteerism.
- The FID has continued to promote civic culture, the acceptance of diversity, conflict management, and principles of citizenship, equality, coexistence, and tolerance. Since its founding twenty years ago, this has been the central work of the department. It is worth mentioning that the FID has achieved impressive results in its various programs, specifically within its young religious leaders' program. The FID's efforts are recognized in public meetings by its many friends in the worlds of government, religion, and civil society.

Community Initiatives in Dialogue and Coexistence
The FID and CEOSS's other departments work on disseminating the principles of citizenship, coexistence, and understanding the "other" in order to promote the creation of a safe space for dialogue between different societal groups separated by religion, gender, geographical scope, and age. This goal was achieved through the adoption of numerous strategies, including the empowering and informing of religious leaders, academic and media professionals, and CSO representatives. With the tools provided by FID and CEOSS, these figures have shown themselves capable of acting as agents of change within their local communities; they are trained and supported in their attempts to plan and implement programs and activities in their communities. In these intercultural discussions, the perspective of the most vulnerable social and cultural groups is presented and their lack of access to dialogue is discussed. These religious and society leaders go on to apply and disseminate what they have learned as part of their own autonomous community initiatives.

Within FID's context, any given community initiative consists of one or multiple sessions of social, cultural, athletic, or artistic activities customized to the needs of the targeted categories (children, youth, women, and others) in order to achieve the goal of the initiative (often associated with dialogue or discussion). Based upon the initiative's duration, it is categorized as follows:

- *Long-term initiatives* are implemented for at least a year, and up to three years. This effort is intended to induce tangible changes on various levels and among different segments of society. It also has an impact on transforming relationships based upon new understandings of the "other," as people are brought together through the values of peace and societal cohesion.
- *Short-term initiatives* are implemented as an activity, or a set of activities, over a period of approximately one week. These short-term initiatives aim to raise awareness on the issues of citizenship, peace, and renunciation of violence. It is worth mentioning that these short-term initiatives often act as sparks that initiate larger and longer-term projects.

The following are three ways of viewing these community initiatives:

- For those *leaders* responsible for preparing and implementing initiatives, community initiatives are the bridge that connects the content of the capacity-building programs in which those leaders participate to the local reality of their communities (addressing issues such as absence of dialogue, manifestations of discrimination, violence, and rejection of the "other"). These initiatives are also regarded as a common space in which leaders can solve problems related to geographical, gender, or religious diversity.
- As for *targeted groups*, including children, youth, teachers, and women, these initiatives are a safe space for those who are religiously different to be introduced, learn from each other, and exchange ideas. It is an opportunity to explore the "other," engage in a dialogue, and break down common stereotypes.
- As for *communities*, initiatives are a means for building community cohesion, reducing violence, and addressing community crises. These efforts also act as a pillar to support local development efforts and keep them from collapsing due to community and social disintegration. Furthermore, these initiatives assist governmental organizations and NGOs – the cultural palaces,[6] CSOs, universities, and so on – in contributing to the enlightenment of the communities they serve by providing a space for them to share and communicate with their constituents, thus serving as an empowerment tool.

---

6. A Cultural Palace is a governmental building and its purpose was to host several types of cultural events, especially artistic events.

Examples of Long-Term Initiatives
1. Origins (Oṣol) Initiative (El-Nikhila Village, Assiut)
In partnership with the Together for Development Association, the Origins Initiative was implemented. The story behind the establishment of this initiative and the selection of this village in particular is worth mentioning in detail.

The concept behind the establishment of Together for Development came from religious leaders, namely Father Matta Shafieq and Sheikh Sayed 'Abd El-'Aziz. Both participated in the FID for many years, eventually going on to join together in their local efforts as members of a community committee in 2005. In 2007, they decided to establish an association to act as a model of joint effort between Muslims and Christians in the village of El-Nikhila. At the time, this locale was experiencing disturbances related to sectarian conflict and incidences of open physical conflict. Moreover, influential families had dominated local matters via the use of tribalism violence, doing so at a cost to other families. El-Nikhila has witnessed significant societal insecurity, religious extremism, and inter-group violence. These events are documented and highlighted in certain artistic works, including the film *Al-Jazera*.

The Together for Development Association, through the Origins Initiative, has sought to formulate a new social contract in El-Nikhila. Moreover, the initiative also aimed at promoting social peace, combating popular violence, and putting an end to conflicts that had emerged due to religious backgrounds or social disparity.

The initiative was launched to promote communal effort to work toward issues that impact all societal convergences – Muslim or Christian, rich or poor – on safe common ground. The initiative called for going back to the village's origin and rediscovering its "Egyptian identity" – an identifier for people best known for their understanding, cooperation, and coexistence.

The initiative targeted four categories of the population: (1) children, (2) youth, (3) women, and (4) leaders.

First, the initiative worked with one hundred and fifty male and female Christian and Muslim children, from 13 to 18 years old. The initiative provided an opportunity for children of different faith backgrounds to be introduced to one other and become closer by working together as part of different awareness-raising cultural activities. This program of the initiative included the following:

- Visits to archaeological sites and places of significant historic events, such as El-Fardous Park, the city of Assiut, and Banque Miṣr. It is worth noting that the involved children were not aware that the founder of Banque Miṣr, Tal'at Ḥarb, was born in Assiut – nor did

some of the children know of the nationally prominent Banque Miṣr itself, its age, or its status.
- Workshops and collective cultural-awareness-raising meetings, which addressed the following topics: acceptance of the "other," saying "yes" to peace and "no" to violence, rights and legal obligations, and Egyptian heritage.
- The organization of a three-day summer camp under the slogan "My Hands with Yours." The camp aimed at raising children's awareness of the significance of their engagement together, fostering acceptance of one another's religious beliefs and intellectual differences and the general deepening of their relationships via engagement with the camp's daily activities. The camp included a visit to Christian and Islamic archaeological sites in Sohag (such as El ʿAbiad Monastery and Sidi ʿArif Mosque).

Second, the initiative worked with fifty young men from El-Nikhila, from eighteen to twenty-nine years old. This project was focused on the promotion of local values that enable their practitioners to carry out initiatives that reflect the values of volunteering and citizenship. The program included:

- Workshops on Egyptian identity, the differences between human identity and national identity, the issue of citizenship, and related impediments to be overcome.
- Sessions on conflict resolution, the differences between disagreement, difference, and conflict, the language and mechanisms of negotiation, and gender issues.
- Encouragement for Muslim and Christian youth to undertake an initiative together in order to serve their village and improve the conditions of the least privileged portions of the local population. This initiative included work with medical convoys, efforts to raise awareness of the importance of hygiene, and community engagement.

Third, the initiative targeted fifty local women. Sessions were held in order to increase their general knowledge of one another, enhance their social relations, encourage them to engage in integrated activities, and promote their participation in public life as a means of overcoming deeply rooted local traditions. The program included:

- Popular meetings to promote dialogue between women of different backgrounds, held in order to raise their awareness of the importance

of the role of women throughout Egyptian history, issues around raising children, the importance of political engagement in order to activate their roles in public life, volunteering and its importance, and the role of women in combating social traditions and customs that may affect their well-being and societal roles.
- Follow-up dialogue sessions to allow participating women to exchange experiences and discuss challenges significant for women. On Mother's Day, one hundred and five women were invited to celebrate that day together as a collective. Outstanding participants, who played significant roles in the local community, were honored and invited to the dialogue sessions to discuss stories related to their successes and challenges.

Finally, the initiative worked to build the capacity of community leaders, including family leaders, officials of the village council, religious leaders, and women involved in activities in the village. These capacity-building programs were held to face any potential challenges or crises and foster a spirit of cooperation and encourage volunteering to disseminate the values of accepting the other, respecting differences, and engagement in community.

The closing day of the initiative coincided with the International Day for Monuments and Sites; subsequently, a celebration was organized in a local square where all of the residents of El-Nikhila and the surrounding communities participated. This celebration displayed the values that the initiative sought to establish – coexistence and a commitment to common ground. It also promoted effective participation by different groups of villagers and reinforced the value of cherishing their communal identity, heritage, and capacity for partnership. Those who reflect on the agenda of the celebration may become familiar with the creative, intellectual, and cultural diversity of those who participated in the event: the program included films, songs, religious music and performance, a presentation of traditional vocations, and displays of folk dancing.

Despite the challenges faced by those engaged in this initiative – a long history of conflict based on violence and the prevailing tribal culture, attempts to prevent the participation of girls, women, and some sub-tribal groups – the initiative has contributed considerably toward the improvement of community relationships. There was a noted reduction in violence and a reinforcement of local stability, as reflected in the following:
- Promotion of effective and continuous communication and relationship-building between Muslim and Christian villagers. Some

of these participants mentioned that they met and talked for the first time because of the initiative's activities, a fact worth noting given that they live in the same rural village.
- Those sub-initiatives launched by youth participants succeeded in encouraging many villagers to participate in the initiative's efforts, specifically including activities involving a medical convoy (which gave villagers access to medical examinations and testing) and From Home to Home, a sub-initiative that promoted cleaning and distribution of garbage bags to the local citizenry.
- "I am positive and involved," said at least one youth participant.
- Assessed indicators reflect the success of the initiative. A group of local leaders was formed to confront any future crisis, a particularly useful local tool considering that those leaders had gained the necessary skills to solve disputes and manage crises. Furthermore, a hub for information and free legal advice was established to accommodate efforts to manage disputes in legal courts.
- The local group's partnership with state authorities, including the cultural palace, the youth center, and the local governmental unit, worked to activate those entities locally and reinforce the results achieved by the initiative.
- Cadres of women were formed in order to offer a common place for women to engage in dialogue and exchange experiences – an important social and cultural tool, given that women's involvement in public life is not a common affair in rural Egypt despite the parliamentary victories of women in other parts of the country.

2. Working Together to Strengthen the Values of Citizenship and a Culture of Tolerance (Menbal Village, Matai District, Minya)

Menbal is a village located in the western region of Minya's Matai District, a region of Upper Egypt. Most of the village's population works in agriculture, while others are employees of local companies or entrepreneurs. Like other villages in Egypt, the low levels of education and lack of exposure to cultural matters outside of their own provided an appropriate environment for its residents to experience sectarian tension.

In 2013, hostile social and political events began to occur; as a result, the FID began to involve a group of local leaders from Menbal in different initiatives meant to help soothe tensions. These efforts allowed the leaders to develop an appreciation for cross-cultural activities and pro-dialogue interventions have supported dialogue among the different populations of the community: Muslims, Christians, adolescents and teens, children, and women. These leaders were also exposed to the problem-solving nature of these initiatives and agreed that such activities would help divert future crises threatening peace and stability in the village. Initially, the idea of the effort emerged from a committee formed from prominent community members such as the sheikh of the village's central mosque, a local priest, the mayor of Menbal village, influential families, teachers, and officers at the village's youth center.

The initiative aimed to raise the awareness of youth, children, and local leaders of the values of citizenship, the importance of disseminating a culture of tolerance and accepting the "other" in the village. The initiative targeted four hundred citizens – primarily youth, children, and local leaders – and took place in public gathering places such as the local youth center and primary education schools. Activities have included artistic and athletic activity sessions, as well as camp events and discussion groups.

The students enrolled at basic education schools, as well as those taking part in classes at primary and preparatory schools, were organized to participate in four local festivals as part of the greater initiative. These festivals included songs, puppet theatre, performance art, drawing activities, and kinetic art sessions. These activities were hosted by multiple local parties; for instance, performances were delivered by artistic staff employed by the cultural palace. Students not only took part in these activities, they also generated their own pieces and performed them for those assembled. All of the observed performances conveyed messages and ideas pertaining to the values of citizenship and accepting the "other."

Teachers and social workers took part via a series of discussions and trainings. These sessions were focused on means by which educators and social service staff can act to deepen the values of a diverse citizenship among their students; participants also took part in capacity-building activities regarding problem-solving on a cultural level, as well as the organization of activities that supported an inclusive culture.

Twenty-five youth – Muslim and Christian, male and female – were trained to initiate and coordinate dialogue; additionally, their communication skills were reinforced by relevant activities. After the trainings, discussions were held among youth about development issues in the village and how they could be solved. The youth reported that, as a result of their participation in these sessions, they were encouraged to be engaged in dialogue about the village's common challenges. A number of issues relevant to agriculture, irrigation, and the availability of fertilizers were raised as part of this discussion; consequently, the participating youth were able to communicate with local officials as a step toward finding a solution to these problems. This effort has contributed to the "building of bridges" between young members of the community on one hand, and between youth and local decision-makers on the others. A group of youth has since invited their Christian and Muslim peers to participate in sports games and camp events that focus on environmental action and artistic endeavors as a means of improving their village.

At the beginning of these efforts, the initiative was adopted by a small group of leaders in the village. This collective succeeded in their efforts to include other prominent members of the community to form a "committee of the wise." The formation of this committee took gender and age into consideration: subsequently, women and young people were represented by individuals who joined the committee. In addition, a religiously diverse group of faith leaders (both Muslim and Christian) and the mayor – as well as some elders of influential local families – took part as full members of this committee. This committee has functioned as a "safety valve": they exert distinct effort to raise awareness and engage in rapid responses to imminent issues between local families or youth to prevent the outbreak of community or sectarian crises. The committee members were keen to offer condolences to locals, participating in weddings and feasts without discrimination between Muslim and Christian. It is worth mentioning that, although the initiative has since formally ended, the members of the "committee of the wise" are still keen to meet and work together as Muslims and Christians, setting a positive example for Menbal village.

The initiative has built up an atmosphere of trust and good relations between Menbal village's Muslims and Christians. The priest and the sheikh – both members of the committee – jointly filed an appeal to the educational district of Matai in order to receive permission to implement the initiative's activities in local schools. This appeal stemmed from inactivity on the part of the local schools' executive management, who have refused to engage in order to avoid the potential for unrest between Muslim and Christian students. The director of the educational district approved this appeal and selected a group of teachers and social workers to coordinate with the committee and develop activities for students.

This appeal was filed by a representative of the association of El-Amir Tadros, the local priest, and Mr Ḥussein Gad, the imam of Menbal village's central mosque, to allow the association to work with the FID, and to implement activities to raise awareness among students, cultivate a local spirit of loyalty and belonging, instil tolerance through cultural sessions, trips, and camps, and reinforce the abilities of local students to avoid having them drop out of school. The district education director approved of this plan, in totality.

Participants have testified to the effectiveness of this initiative:[7]

- Kastor Labib, a Christian student in grade 9, participated and benefited from the activities of the initiative. She reported that, prior to taking part in these sessions, "[she] didn't feel comfortable sitting beside any Muslim student, or going together to private tutoring." She also added that her family had advised her to avoid dealing with Muslims. "The activities of the initiatives and meetings organized by the school helped me to approach my Muslim colleagues. We have drawn and made paintings together on the meaning of citizenship."
- Maḥamoud, a Muslim young man, reported:

    I haven't dealt with or sat beside a Christian. I prefer dealing with Muslims instead of Christians. I have participated in a camp that one Muslim colleague asked me to attend. The camp was full of mutual activities between Muslim and Christian youth. At the beginning, I felt that these activities weren't in compliance with my beliefs and ideas; however, dialogue and participation in mutual activities have changed the image I had in my mind. It helped me to understand my Christian colleague, particularly when I saw the imam and the priest participate and talk together. I wish that such type of initiatives continues to reach the larger number of youths.

After the involvement of the FID, the initiative continued on a self-supporting basis; the committee continued working diligently with governmental organizations that supported the initiative, and the local unit has opened its doors for regular meetings held to raise citizens' awareness of issues in Menbal village. The cultural palace has organized cultural and artistic sessions for youth and school students, and their efforts are supplemented by efforts made by the local youth center to organize sports games and youth camps for both Muslims and Christians.

3. Communication Initiative (Aswan, Upper Egypt)

Aswan is one of the five governorates that form the southern region of Upper Egypt. It is approximately 879 kilometers south of the capital of Cairo and

---

7. Quotes are direct testimonials from initiative participants.

includes five sub-districts with a total size of 400 square kilometers. It is a governorate possessing great ethnic and tribal diversity, home to diverse groups such as the Nuba, El-Ga'fara, El-'Abassein, El-Anṣar, El-Abiada, El-Bashyra, El-Hilel, and El-Dabodia. Some of the aforementioned tribes are descended from Arab origins, while others have Nubian origins. Additionally, there exist groups that have arrived in Aswan from other Egyptian governorates.

It is a paradox that a region of such cultural enrichment and diversity – manifested in its arts, languages, marriage customs, food, and other cultural aspects – can contribute to clan loyalties that may negatively impact local stability and peace. In Aswan, such loyalty was present during local parliamentary elections: each tribe or ethnic group wished to see their nominee win, as they believed that a nomination of one of "their own" could increase their power in comparison to other local groups.

Additionally, local issues between different clan groups in Aswan have shown themselves to have the capacity to spiral into full-blown crises. In 2014, minor conflicts between youth belonging to the El-Dabodia and Bani Hilel tribes spiraled into a spate of local violence that led to the death of twenty-three people – an explicit and painful image of what results from tribal fanaticism. Many of those who were accused of taking part in these acts of violence were subsequently sentenced to jail or were issued the death penalty. These events naturally affected all of Aswan's inhabitants – particular the youth, as they became easy targets for vengeful actions as well as ready participants in subsequent violence.

After these events, the Community Development Association and the Consumer Protection Association – a local agency (and member organization of the FID) that has, among other objectives, a goal of disseminating an ideology of peace and coexistence – launched a small initiative called Colors. This effort was conceived in partnership with CEOSS and area youth centers that had witnessed the 2014 tribal violence. The initiative targeted juveniles and youth, who were provided with a number of youth center activities of an artistic, cultural, or social focus. A group of youth was equipped and prepared to be leaders of local trainings regarding citizenship and coexistence.

While evaluating the impact of this initiative, the two local associations and CEOSS agreed upon the importance of working with Aswan's youth on a larger scale. Within a new initiative, it was decided that the youth should be the main actors in disseminating the values of peace and coexistence, responsible for urging their communities to renounce violence and fanaticism by providing positive examples. Subsequently, these youth designed an initiative called Liaison, an effort named to represent what they hoped to be for their communities. The project focused on training a small group of youth on the values of citizenship, dialogue, the renunciation of violence, and peacebuilding. The individual members of this initial cadre would act as the primary liaisons with other groups of youth to convey to them these same essential societal values. From these secondary groups, new liaisons would emerge to serve an even greater portion of Aswan's youth population. These youth made great efforts to raise Aswan's public awareness of the values of peace and coexistence through artistic activities, camps sessions, and other sub-initiatives.

After its inception, the initiative selected Aswan University to be a prominent local partner. A protocol was signed between the university and the partnering associations, pledging expert support from the university's specialized professors for assistance in this endeavor. Since the signing of the protocol, Aswan University has participated in selecting outstanding students and assisting them in reaching youth groups through university activities and student unions across the eighteen faculties of Aswan University. A committee of representatives has been formed, consisting of university figures and local leaders, to provide additional support to youth efforts within the community.

The initiative accomplished the following:

- Thirty young men and women were empowered in many faculties and institutes to develop their aptitudes related to community dialogue and the concept of coexistence through a training program developed and delivered in cooperation with experts from Aswan University and human development specialists. These young men and women were selected due to their professional and academic focuses being in close alignment with the initiative's focus. Particular topics of relevance were the faculties of arts, specifically education and social services. Ten youth who had received training via the Colors Initiative joined these sessions as well.
- Initiative-coordinated youth cadres planned and implemented twenty-four interactive activities amongst university students to better disseminate the principles of coexistence. These activities included the painting of murals, showings of a film entitled *Mobile*, the holding of public service camps, storytelling workshops, and theatre activities at the cultural salon, and the conducting of related research. It is worth mentioning that the target participation number for these activities, according to the youth plan, was four hundred male and female students; the actual number of male and female students that participated, however, exceeded seven hundred.

- Groups of students implemented sessions focused on awareness-raising initiatives relevant to the matters of coexistence and acceptance of the "other"; these sessions took place off-campus and were aimed at the local non-university population. The coordinating groups worked with youth centers to hold dialogue sessions and workshops for youth who visit the centers. They also organized camps for participants and hosted theatrical performances in coordination with the cultural palace.
- Involved youth concluded their efforts with local community members by painting a civil values mural in the main tunnel that links the different parts of Aswan – a location that thousands of residents pass through on a daily basis. Many commuters are now privy to a display that expresses the values of coexistence and the acceptance of diversity. The piece also incorporates slogans that call for working together, helping one another, and building social peace. It should be mentioned that the involved youth and the coordinating CBO conducted a campaign of community mobilization in order to paint this mural and also communicated with a number of important procedural figures – including representatives of Minya Governorate and the local governmental unit and several prominent businessmen – in order to gain the requisite legal permissions and material resources needed to accomplish this initiative.
- Since the inauguration of this initiative, the administration of Aswan University has supported the efforts of select student groups and has provided them with on-campus facilities in which to carry out their activities and workshops (at no charge). High-profile university leaders – namely, an academic dean – have participated in sessions and attended student performances. In addition, the Institute of Social Service has since conducted research on the value of coexistence.
- In order to disseminate the initiative as a model of communication and coexistence among local youth, Aswan's Future Association filmed a documentary that showcased the initiative and captured the impact the events had upon involved youth, including success stories from its participants. The documentary was uploaded onto social media and received a high number of views; it was also broadcast prominently on the Tiba Channel, the regional channel for southern Upper Egypt.

4. The Together on the Road Initiative (Luxor)
In partnership with the Nour Al-Islam (light of Islam) Charity Association, this long-term initiative was conducted by the FID in Luxor, a city located in southern Upper Egypt, for almost two consecutive years.

The idea for this initiative emerged in 2015, shortly after the dramatic social, political and cultural changes that took place in Egypt, which greatly impacted society and resulted in the manifestation of violence across some communities, families, classes, denominations, and age groups. This was the case in Sharq El-Ḥadid, Luxor – an informal urban area with high population density, low economic wealth, reduced social prosperity, and a high rate of residential casual laborers. In this locale, sporadic violence became prevalent among young people and children of "opposing" groups. Luxor's Social Education Department recorded many incidences of conflict between students of different educational levels, particularly in the preparatory setting, and taking place predominantly between students living east of the city's railway. These conflicts developed as a result of differences between religious groups, as Christians and Muslims attempted to find fault with and initiate violence against the other. Ethnic and tribal differences also negatively influenced this matter: it was reported that some students belonging to certain tribal groups had planned to act out against others in the case of conflict.

The Nour El-Islam Association had a mandate to enact positive interventions that would contribute to a reduction in the number of these inter-group incidents and the prevalence of violence in the area east of the railway. As a result, Nour El-Islam communicated with the FID committee – a group consisting of local religious leaders and intellectuals – situated in Luxor. The committee and CEOSS worked together to develop "Together on the Road," an initiative that aimed to bolster the culture of coexistence and the principles of dialogue among children, youth, and women. Additionally, "Together on the Road" sought to enable local leaders to act as seeds disseminating the values of inter-group acceptance, respect for the "other," protection of the community in times of crises, and resistance against acts of violence. The initiative engaged in the following specific interventions:

- It raised awareness in basic education schools using storytelling workshops. Sixty students, eight to twelve years old, were selected and divided into two groups based upon their ages. Storytelling workshops were held, giving children the opportunity to share stories of troublesome incidents in their respective communities and discuss solutions to reduce and eliminate violence. For each session, the coordinator collected all the stories and combined them into one narrative. The participating children then "translated" this story into drawings and cartoons to be added to a combined coloring booklet. The booklet was provided to all school students, and events to engage them with the work were held. The booklet produced by the children was published and used by more than one thousand students.

- Forty young teachers and youth center employees were trained to better instill the values of peace and coexistence among their young students. They were also trained in handling common crises and problems present in schools and youth centers. Numerous events were organized to support communication among youth and children as a result of these trainings, including the viewing and discussing of films, trainings on mobile cinema, and events centered around the designing and painting of murals.
- A "committee of the wise" was established to be responsible for rapid intervention regarding any local crises before they worsened. Twenty religious leaders, representatives of Dandara Cultural Center, and other influential local leaders were selected and trained in communication and dispute resolution. The committee of the wise has since held regular meetings.
- A council consisting of twenty-five women was formed in Luxor, specifically to activate women's community engagement and enhance the role of women in promoting a culture of peace and the confrontation of violence. In coordination with the National Council for Woman in Luxor, the parliament conducted a door-to-door campaign to raise awareness on the values of coexistence and community solidarity. The campaign targeted one thousand people (two hundred families). The parliament has also analyzed the social and cultural needs of Luxor to proactively design and implement an action plan that could contribute to the meeting of those needs. This action plan will be conducted in coordination with the government, NGOs, and CSOs.

The positive impact of this initiative can be seen through two major ongoing factors: (1) in regards to the development of its coordinators' relationships with partner organizations and (2) via the testimonies of the project's beneficiaries and local partners.

Regarding the first of these factors, the partnership between CEOSS (a Christian organization) and the Nour El-Islam Association (a Muslim organization) has proved the possibility that Muslims and Christians can work together to positively impact the community of Luxor. This partnership initially raised many questions from individuals and organizations, many of whom joined the initiative's early activities out of curiosity to learn about this partnership. These participants had their attitude changed once they realized that the basis of this partnership was a mutual agreement upon the significance of community cohesion and peace. Thus, this partnership focused on the human being regardless of religion, gender, or belief.

At the beginning of the project, many schools refused the request to implement interventions in their schools; thus, the committee of wise and the partners communicated directly with the educational district. At the beginning, the initiative worked with only two schools. By the end of the initiative, the association received a "thank-you" letter from the educational district and a request to extend this project to cover fourteen schools.

The partnerships developed can be further seen in the success of the committee of the wise in ending a sectarian tension that occurred in El-Mahidat village. This issue arose as a result of a relationship between a Christian girl and a Muslim young man, which led to violence between the two associated families. The committee communicated with some local leaders and parliament members, held meetings with the two families, and were able to reach an agreement that didn't impact the accountability of any perpetrators of violence (this last factor being the responsibility of local security figures).

Regarding the second of these factors, the following are examples of testimonies from project beneficiaries and local partners:

- The principal of El-Salam School (a partner education facility) reported that the school's students used to fight regularly amongst themselves; after carrying out the activities of the initiative, however, the occurrence of these events decreased dramatically.
- A student mentioned that he used to be violent and to beat his peers when they disagreed with him. After attending the workshops, he learned that violence causes more violence and that dialogue is a more productive option.
- A young man reported that the project has contributed to building his character. This was reflected in his new ability to express his thoughts towards many topics and issues.

- A woman reported that attending the women's workshops encouraged her to be more engaged in society. She expressed her intention to run for the local council elections.
- A social worker who received training stated that the training has helped improve his ability to solve students' problems and has enabled him to engage with students more professionally.
- The students of Najʿ El-Qabaḥy School (a partner educational facility) have admirably displayed the values they learned in the workshops at the school showcase. They have designed paintings that express positive social values and have hung their art in their classrooms to better convey what they have learned to their peers.

5. Bashayer Khair Initiative (Ṣaft El-Laben Village, Minya)

Ṣaft El-Laben is an agriculturally oriented village that has a high percentage of inhabitants with an advanced level of education, receiving certification from either middle educational facilities or higher. The community also hosts schools, a nursery, a local health unit, a youth center, and multiple NGOs. These organizations merely existing does not mean that they are effective, however – and this matter is exacerbated further due to the locale's clear sectarian divisions. Christians are concentrated on the northern side of the village, while Muslims are concentrated on the southern side of the village. This division is due to family relations, long-term land ownership, and economic reasons. Locally, Christians possess more economic strength as they own most of the local agricultural lands and are a prominent influence on the local crop markets.

Occasionally, violence and fights erupt in the Ṣaft El-Laben village. It is worth mentioning that, prior to any initiative-based work, there was no communication or dialogue between the place's different groups on any level – particularly between Muslims and Christians. There was an urgent need to establish and strengthen the community's capacity for communication, as such a change could protect the village against future sectarian conflict.

A partnership was established between CEOSS and El-Maḥaba Charity Association. From this pairing, the Bashayer Khair plan (meaning "first fruits of the harvest") was developed and implemented. This plan aimed at building up a culture of dialogue, enhancing the values of community cohesion, and a strong effort to increase the acceptance of "the other" in Ṣaft El-Laben.

CEOSS called for the formation of a community committee of religious leaders, the mayor, the families' elders, representatives of some local organizations including teachers, and officials of the youth center. If created, this committee would be mandated with supporting the planning and implementation of the initiative. The formation of this committee was not an easy task, as many Muslim leaders refused to participate and publicly expressed their belief that the initiative would not be fruitful. These figures also believed that they would not play a leading role on the committee, due to the existing local disparity of power; however, Christian leaders communicated with them and explained the significance of the initiative in a manner that established trust. CEOSS reinforced this effort by providing development incentivizing agricultural services for poor Christians and Muslims – a common ground that paved the way for working together in the Bashayer Khair initiative.

CEOSS has built the planning and preparing capacities of the committee so as to be prepared for each stage of the initiative. For two and a half years, all of the committee's participants have taken part in training sessions with CEOSS staff members and have also contributed to the planning and implementation of the greater initiative. In 2019, the first phase of the initiative was put into effect.

The initiative has achieved the following:

- Raised the awareness of two hundred residents of Ṣaft El-Laben on the issues of citizenship and coexistence by holding culturally oriented events, included chanting and music, in order to highlight that Egyptian identity accepts all different religious denominations. On national days (for example, the historical victory of the October 6 War), performances under the title of "From Egypt, and We Love Egypt" were held to develop and reinforce a spirit of kinship among Muslims and Christians.
- Sixty Muslim and Christian women were provided with knowledge and skills on the values of citizenship and understanding the importance of respecting the "other." They developed these abilities in order to better convey such values to their children and colleagues at their workplaces. The initiative enhanced their ability to disseminate these values in the community by holding discussion sessions.
- Used different types of arts in order to improve the level of awareness and conduct of young people (aged twelve to eighteen) regarding a culture of tolerance and inter-group acceptance. As part of the initiative, a festival was held for two hundred children. Its associated events contained cultural, artistic, and athletic activities meant to enhance communication between Christian and Muslim children in the village. Visits were organized to monumental sites, including

Tel El-Amarna and Bani Hassen, to introduce children to Egyptian civilization and promote a focus on their Egyptian identity. Four storytelling and arts workshops were held in partnership with the Egypt Public Library, the Minya Cultural Palace, and the staff of Alwanat Company for Arts and Culture. These events were presented to eighty children and were focused on the values of renouncing violence and accepting one another. Furthermore, the initiative focused on developing the children's talents, and a choir of thirty children was formed. Its participants were trained on composing and singing nationalist songs that promoted messages of unity and peace.

- Empowered and built the capacity of ninety young men, eighteen to thirty years old, in the field of dialogue, inter-group acceptance, and coexistence via training and discussion sessions. These events were attended by both Muslims and Christians and included a range of activities, including cleanliness camps, ecological activities such as the planting of trees, and drawing murals on the streets of Ṣaft El-Laban that express unity and community cohesion (completed in cooperation with the students of fine arts and art education faculties). One hundred and forty young men and women also participated in related sports and artistic competitions. Furthermore, thirty Muslim and Christian young men and women paid visits to the Historical Religious Complex. It was the first time these Muslim youth had visited a church, and the first time that the Christians had attended a mosque.

- Empowered and strengthened a committee of local and executive leaders to contribute to the promoting of community peace and the resolving of disputes (as learned through associated training events). Participants also gained the skills necessary to manage crises and engage in community peace-building. Those leaders went on to conduct a door-to-door campaign with the support of religious leaders, which raised awareness on the importance of coexistence for eighty families. The campaign included visits to families and the exchanging of greetings on religious and national occasions.

Many of those who participated in these efforts reported positive engagement with its associated activities. Some of their comments are as follows:

- Ayman Ibrahim, youth center officer: "For the first time in the youth center, there was a sports competition between Muslim and Christian youth. They played as one team, with one spirit."

- Sheikh Imam Moḥsen (imam of the mosque in Ṣaft El-Laben): "Having religious leaders [taking part in this initiative] has contributed to the building of trust among youth."
- Oshean ʿAdel (a young woman participating in the initiative): "This is the first time for me to enter a mosque. It was a good opportunity for me to be introduced to the other and change the image I had in my mind."
- Amana Aḥmed saʿid: "I was outstanding in accomplishing assignments individually. I haven't participated in any social activities – but the initiative made me more positive and effective. I have a role!"
- ʿAtef Aḥmed (school principal and member of the community committee) stated that using art and drawing, as well as the cultural visits, have assisted in removing barriers among children.

Examples of Short-Term Initiatives
1. Keyboard Initiative, El-Maḥaba – El-Moqattam, Cairo

The El-Moqattam neighborhood of Cairo is known for the diversity of its residents, in terms of social and economic standards. In El-Moqattam, rich inhabitants live in villas; on the other hand, those disadvantaged populations displaced from home collapses – a long-term result of a 1992 earthquake – reside in an area referred to as the "Earthquake Dwellings." The poor sub-neighborhood is known for its low social mobility, cultural restrictions, and reduced educational standards. El-Moqattam witnessed many incidences of violence, particularly after the January Revolution and the rule of the Muslim Brotherhood. This violence took many forms, including violence between youth and violence against women.

In 2011, the Evangelical Church in Moqattam formed an association called the Love Group. This entity consisted of religious leaders and community members – especially those recognized for their moderation and wisdom – willing to take responsibility for opening the channels of communication and improving relationships between Muslims and Christians and between the poor and the rich. This group began its work by having breakfast together once a month. They used the breakfast to meet, exchange their viewpoints, and engage in constructive dialogue. Each time the group members met for breakfast, they were keen to invite new participants – particularly youth and women – to participate with them. After establishing familiarity, participants began autonomously enacting local initiatives: for example, planting the gardens of the mosque and the gardens of the church with trees and organizing entertainment-oriented events for local families to attend.

In partnership with FID, the Love Group implemented an initiative for eight- to twelve-year-old children in order to contribute to the creation of a new generation inspired by the values of peace and acceptance of the "other."

Those responsible for this initiative found that the best way to attract children to participate in its events was technology – namely, computers. As a result, the coordinators named it the Keyboard Initiative: a model in which the keys of a computer keyboard would be discussed allegorically, each key representing an important message or value. The "Escape" key represented an escape from negative thoughts held about other groups, while the combination of the "Alt" and "Shift" keys signified a change in attitude; "Backspace" represented stepping away from conflict, and "Enter" stood for the beginning of a new idea or project phase.

The initiative worked with two hundred boys and girls of different religious and social backgrounds. Participants met for three sessions, over the course of three days, to engage in activities and play games together. Their slogan, "We have different shapes, natures and opinions, but when it comes to our country we are sisters and brothers and should agree together," acts to accurately represent the values promoted by the initiative. Many performances and short videos generated by the participants reflected a value or positive attitude inspired by the initiative, and they were uploaded for public consumption on YouTube. The initiative has also organized competitions, sports leagues, and meaningful gaming sessions.

This initiative was very simple in terms of direct interventions and timeframe, as it was implemented for just three days. However, its impact cannot be overstated: although completed in a short period of time, the initiative gave children an opportunity to express the change that took place in their lives before and after their participation. Their words reflect profound positivity:

- "We are different in everything, except for one thing: that we are all human beings. This is why we have to respect and handle each other with love."
- "God has created us differently, not to quarrel and fight, but to use our different characteristics to live with each other."
- "Actually, I didn't use to deal with people who aren't my type. I learned that if I continue this attitude, I'll be alone. So, I decided to accept all people regardless of the fact that they are different from me."
- "I have taught my neighbors the slogan, and we sing it together daily."

2. Marathon, Youth Who Combat Violence and Discrimination (Alexandria)

The following are the words of a group of youth from Alexandria who were responsible for coordinating this initiative:

> This initiative was designed in a training delivered by CEOSS. In the training, there was a discussion about the most prevailing issues in our community. The majority of participants agreed that violence prevailed in Alexandria, which was also an urgent issue. Accordingly, we decided to launch an initiative that included raising awareness in an innovative way. We called it "Youth combating violence, extremism, and discrimination" to be carried out in the neighborhoods of Gomrok, Abies and Cornish for three days. Following are the partners of the initiatives: CEOSS, The House of the Egyptian Family, bicycle Miṣr, Serjacko Egypt, and the management of El-Gomrok neighborhood.
>
> The purpose of the initiative was to raise awareness of the necessity of combating violence and refusing all shapes of discrimination (men and women, Muslim and Christian, Upper Egypt residents, rural inhabitants and urban inhabitants). It also aimed at putting an end to extremism and enhancing the value of community engagement. The youth who were responsible for the initiative thought that they had to use non-traditional methods to raise awareness. This is why they have selected the bike marathon on Friday at Alexandria Cornish. They communicated with media professionals in order to highlight the idea. They distributed roles on the team and also identified the needed tasks from each member. In addition, they have defined the organizations that will participate and support this marathon.

This initiative resulted in attracting the attention of Alexandrian society and making people more receptive to its core values of accepting the "other" and coexistence. The events of the initiative generated a number of positive interactions that made the group that implemented the initiative, the Alexandrian youth, very happy with their initiative idea. Many Alexandrians have inquired with the participants about the initiative and how they could participate in more similar activities.

The Alexandria Running Team's training coincided with the preparations for the marathon; as a result, some of its members inquired about the initiative and suggested the organization of a running marathon under the name of the initiative. Moreover, some of them joined the initiative's bike marathon.

The success of this initiative could be attributed to personal relationships, governate leaders' belief in the initiative, the ability of those responsible for the initiative to find more similar activities, and the harmony among participants. On the other hand, there were many opportunities available for the initiative including that this initiative was carried out on Friday, the weekend.

3. "The Dialogue Continues" Initiative: A Radio Program on the Values of Citizenship and Coexistence

Young media professionals are key partners in the FID. Accordingly, CEOSS built up the capacities of these individuals and provided them with requisite knowledge and skills relevant to the values of citizenship and coexistence. These skills were developed in workshops based on interaction, discussion, and the exchanging of experiences, with a focus on using the media to promote positive values and improve the means by which the members of society engage with related issues.

Participants were encouraged to adopt initiatives that reflected their understanding and concern, while also applying what they had learned to their places of work. In this regard, a committee of young media professionals launched a radio program initiative that consisted of thirty episodes. This series was broadcast over the month of Ramadan. These episodes discussed values including citizenship, community peace, diversity, and understanding one another across cultural lines. Each episode contained a semi-drama, presented in a comic way, followed by an interview with an intellectual or youth, and some episodes concluded with comments from listeners on the values discussed in the episode and their importance in Egyptian society. This initiative was carried out for two consecutive years and was broadcast on Sout El-Arab (voice of the Arabs) – the oldest radio station in Egypt and the Middle East, boasting a high percentage of consistent listeners.

4. Enabling Youth to Coexist and Community Engagement (Bani Suef Governorate)

It is evident that youth in Egypt in general, and in the Bani Suef Governorate in particular, are very socially active. Often, however, they have societal misconceptions – or, according to others, unclear civic principles. Youth often benefit from having their efforts organized in order for their impact to be felt positively in their community. Subsequently, an initiative was launched by a group of youth leaders associated with the FID and implemented in partnership with Bani Suef's Nile Center for Media. The project aimed to enhance youth community engagement by building the capacities of its participants on the concepts of democracy, engagement, acceptance of the "other," and dialogue.

The initiative targeted young men and women. The Directorate of Youth and Sports, the Directorate of Education, local media figures, representatives of the Department of Endowment, and church leaders also participated in this initiative.

Over four weeks (the duration of the initiative), the following was accomplished:

- A survey was conducted to better know the opinions of the participating youth in regard to the topics of the training. The survey showed that the topics of priority were engagement, citizenship, acceptance of the "other," managing disagreement, and peace-building. The initiative utilized a simulated model of coexistence in order to develop the participants' familiarity with each training topic.
- The initiative implemented three main activities: the organizing of a training camp (hosting physical, athletic, and artistic activities) for fifty young men and women, meant to promote the initiative's central values. These fifty initial participants were trained to convey the positive civic messages learned during their time in the initiative. Each of the participants followed up by teaching another ten young men or women, leading to approximately five hundred young people being impacted by the program.
- Youth participants produced a play entitled *Watch Your Tongue*. This work was performed at the theatres of the university and the cultural palace. These performances were attended by approximately one thousand young men and women. An associated competition for creating oil paintings and drawings expressing the values of tolerance and peace was also held.

The initiative's impacts have been observed as significant, as seen below:

- The initiative has helped to eliminate conflicts between participating youth and religious leaders. It has also decreased the likelihood of person-to-person conflict between groups, in part due to the constructive participation of the aforementioned religious leaders.
- Five youth centers and sports clubs had their roles activated in order to serve as resource centers for civic education. Additionally, the director of the Youth and Sports Directorate allocated 10 percent of their funds to the youth and sports centers engaged in ongoing civic education.

5. Ethics in Our Schools (Alexandria)

This initiative was planned and implemented by nine young men and women in Alexandria who attended a one-year training program (as led by the FID) on the values of peace, citizenship, overcoming violence, and combating discrimination. Its coordinators launched this initiative in order to promote the values that they learned as part of their experiences with the FID. Its coordinators also hoped to strengthen the values of respect, teamwork, tolerance, and a culture of peace among students enrolled in Alexandria's primary schools.

This initiative was implemented in two phases. The first phase began with the hosting of a training for teachers and social workers, as delivered by an education professor from Alexandria University. The professor presented appropriate methods for communicating with students and methods by which to create trust between teachers, social workers, and students and among the student body itself. During the second phase, two-day events for children were conducted by those who had participated in the first phase. At these events, children learned the values of acceptance, cooperation, and dialogue through mentoring and engagement. Activities included:

- Teamwork-based games won by the team that engaged most productively as a unit.
- Visiting the information center in the governorate of Alexandria and being introduced to the initiative implemented by the governorate to face environmental problems. A session was then held with the initiative officer so that children could ask about additional interventions from their own perspectives in order to develop this initiative.
- Hosted by a group of youth specialized in art, a workshop was held for children in order to translate their ideas regarding the environment into paintings and drawings. This event allowed for the children to develop their creativity and freedom to express themselves.
- A visit was paid to Bibliotheca Alexandria, where the children were able to visit the planetarium and other departments within the Bibliotheca. The participating children were thus introduced to modern scientific ideas and exposed to various new experiences.
- Every child who participated in the initiative was asked to express a value that they learned from the initiative via the mediums of drawing or writing. The children's drawings expressed the values that

they had learned in the initiative, including teamwork, honesty, and cooperation. Collectively, the children have also agreed that these values should be promoted in their schools.

The Impact of CEOSS

To summarize, I posit that CEOSS has been successful in its ability to process the basic principles of modern developmental thought in order to best adapt such practices to the Egyptian context. To best serve the many diverse segments of Egyptian society, CEOSS has become entrenched in a field requiring dedication, pragmatism, resource management, and the ability to act beyond mere theory. In addition, CEOSS has shown an ability to adapt and change its efforts with both "the times" and "the needs": as Egyptian society changes, CEOSS has shown a capacity to change alongside it.

Through an assessment of the most local developmental efforts, it becomes evident that each action – small or large, community-based or individually-targeted – has the potential to deeply and positively affect multiple Egyptian lives. Protecting and preserving the well-being of working children or street children enhances their ability to engage in education, civic life, family life, and greater Egyptian culture; following up on preventative initiatives related to eyesight or visual ability, too, allows for medically-disadvantaged Egyptians to more fully participate in society. Customized initiatives for people with special needs have helped foster both the physical and social statuses of disabled Egyptians. With proper assistance from sustainable development programs, disabled Egyptians are educated and empowered to the point where participation in social and vocational settings is more than just a possibility. Far from a rhetorical slogan, CEOSS's extensive work empowering women in the face of violence has become an urgent and practical societal necessity.

These efforts reinforce the importance of faith-based civil society organizations in Egypt. In the case of CEOSS, we see religious values extensively utilized to enrich Egyptian society.

As observed, both the cultural and developmental initiatives of CEOSS act as extensions of the ethics, culture, and morals that empower such an organization. As seen throughout Egypt and the greater Middle East, religion continues to represent an amazing force that – when applied directly and knowledgeably to society's ills – can have an undoubtedly constructive influence.

6

Conclusion

It is important to recognize the significant changes within Egypt's political, social, and religious spheres within the last five decades, especially in the context of assessing how and why such elements impacted the church. Several factors – political, social, and cultural – did indeed contribute to a disconnection between Christians and greater Egyptian society. Prominent among such factors was the role played by political Islam, a complex ideology which maximized the discontinuity between the typical Christian and Egyptian experiences; as political Islam rose to social and political prominence, Christians subsequently experienced a distinct cultural and social isolation. These and other related events led to a "discontinuation" of the church in public life; over time, continuing shifts in those same fields of society led to the church's eventual re-emergence and return to active engagement with Egyptian society.

Attempts were made over the years to build bridges across the river that disconnected the average Christian and the average Egyptian. Such efforts met with little success, especially within the context of a totalitarian political system and a weakened civil society. After the January 25 and June 30 Revolutions, however, major shifts allowed for new types of communication. The second revolution stands out as an event that brought all spectrums of Egyptian society together – including the Christians – as a mobilized, engaged faction within national politics. The rise and fall of political Islam in Egypt helped usher in a new period of Christian civic engagement: Christians were allowed – and urged, even – to claim and prove their place within the political, social, and economic fields. After decades of isolation, Copts set out to participate in society at all levels. As Christians themselves began to participate openly in civil society, the church, too, entered into a state of resurgence. We see that the relationship between church and society was, and is, not static; rather, it has always been a dynamic relationship that changes and evolves alongside political and social events. These changes have the capacity to lead to the building of bridges between groups and can enhance societal communication; alternatively, such shifts can also contribute to the building of walls between peoples and usher in the arrival of new discontinuity.

That is why we emphasized that what happened in the June 30 Revolution of 2013 was a great national event that brought all spectrums of society together, including the Christians as an effective national faction in political life. Finally, after decades of isolation, the Christians set out to participate in society on all levels. Also, the June 30 Revolution was an invitation for Christians to return once again to influence society in various fields. Because of this glorious revolution, Christians today have an active presence in the political, social, and economic scene.

In our examination of the relationship between the church and society, we faced a number of profound questions. Who should initiate efforts meant to enhance communication with "the other," the community or the church? If such initiatives are taken up by the community, what kind of supplemental role should the church play? Keeping in mind the focus of this work, the most pressing question still remains: should preaching be the priority and focus of the institutional church, or should the institutional church look to earthly matters as well? Should the church exert all possible efforts to achieve justice, lift up those affected by injustice, promote social equality (especially for marginalized groups), and fight for every change that needs to be made? Eschatological matters, too, are central to these queries. Should the church focus more closely upon the eternal salvation of the human soul?

In this work, I have provided an overview of several theses generated by influential theologians; from these theses, I have assessed three models of mission. These models are potentially representative of the "whole works" of the church and may naturally vary depending upon the general context in which the institutional church exists. The three models are as follows:

- The first model, in which the church seeks to focus on outwardly preaching the message of the gospel, the deeper theological content of the gospel, and the essential nature of human salvation.
- The second model, in which the church promotes the message of the gospel by manifesting the content of such a message in a practical and socially engaged manner.
- The third model (the integral and holistic model), in which the church outwardly preaches the message of the gospel while also

striving to manifest this message via community involvement and societal engagement.

In assessing these models, I emphasized the importance of a theology of transparency. Such a theology remains fundamental to the role of the church: good works cannot be performed under the shadow of a hidden agenda, especially when one's own theology emphasizes the importance of accountable, honest engagement with society. I must stress that the church should not ignore its dedication to the promotion of the gospel. This does not mean, however, that the church should engage in such developmental efforts in order to "hunt" or "fish" for new congregants: the social efforts of the church must be undertaken in an honest and transparent fashion.

If the church merges the "social mission" into its very structure and engages in such an effort transparently, civil society takes notice. As we have observed in this book, faith-based civil society organizations have shown a tendency and capacity to deeply engage in "on-the-ground" social and developmental work. With the right commitment and institutional support, the church can directly participate in such efforts. Over time, the church has the opportunity to show itself to be a reliable partner in developmental matters; thus, interactions between the church and civil society become warm, respectful, and constructive despite ideological or theological disagreements.

Based on this theory of integrated and engaged mission, it is natural that the church may seek to promote initiatives that reinforce both the message of the gospel and the role of civil society – and in the Egyptian context, this may come in the form of citizenship. Citizenship is a broad concept that goes well-beyond state membership and political participation to include a citizen's social, cultural, and economic rights. It is these rights – based on and reinforced by the practice of democracy – that truly strengthen civil society. While working to support legal equality is a noble goal, I do not believe it is fully sufficient. I believe that true citizenship represents more than just legal equality: it is its own form of social justice. If such a concept does not "fit" within the greater culture, equality remains a simple legal statute as opposed to a deeply held societal value. Equality in words alone cannot establish citizenship.

From this standpoint, I emphatically stressed the necessity of the church's transparent theological orientation towards the society in which it finds itself. In Egypt, such a controversial relationship continues to develop: as the social-minded civil society grows stronger and begins to work alongside the church, the theological and social missions of the church become essential. The institutional church must play its role effectively and must do so in a manner appropriate to the greater culture in which it exists.

The matter of coexistence, too, weighs heavily upon all involved. Over the course of this book, we explored its contemporary emergence in Egypt – but with careful reading of the Bible, we know that such a concept is deeply rooted within our theology. The story of creation appears to act as a model of pluralism. The divine declaration of partnership across the two covenants, too, contributes to the theological bases for coexistence and pluralism found throughout the Old and New Testaments. Within contemporary Egypt and elsewhere, we have had the privilege to see how coexistence can emerge between parties with different beliefs regardless of these differences.

When doctrinal differences begin to actively hinder a societal preference for coexistence, however, the possibility for conflict looms large. Societies may struggle with these wider issues, but we have seen evidence that peace becomes possible when one person makes the decision to learn to live alongside another person. In doing so, they accept and acknowledge the differences between one another; over time and exposure, they may learn about the lives of "the other" and act to better the condition of their neighbor. In Egypt, sowing the seeds of coexistence has contributed to the openness of Christians toward participation in political and societal life. As we see, the essences of pluralism and coexistence are inextricably linked.

In addressing the church's roles regarding social work and political awareness, I have strongly emphasized the "theology of creation" along with the "theology of redemption." Our understanding of God as the Creator of the world means that God acts as our caretaker for all affairs, be they spiritual or material. Through such caretaking, God is the source of humanity's political and social rights. By virtue of creation, humanity acts as a participant in life and all that comes along with it: food, work, shelter, family, and property. Having received such bounties, each person is transparently responsible before God regarding their relationship with others and their relationship towards the future of the world and future generations. In committing to God's values and engaging with the world around them, each person acts as both a product and steward of God's creation.

Based on these points, I invite the church in Egypt, and everywhere – today more than ever – to live out the theology of transparent engagement in ministry and mission. The church is driven to participate in the struggle to free humanity from social sin: fear, injustice, hunger, and oppression are countered by the church's call for healing and reconciliation, as well as initiatives to meet the needs of the poor, the sick, the marginalized, and the vulnerable. I urge the greater church to strive to fulfill the mission of Christ in spreading justice, peace, and love in our world. The world needs the church to play the role of the Good Samaritan: one who is not concerned with the identity of the wounded "other," but rather heals the other's wounds, relieves the other's pain, and renews the other's life.

It is my hope that the worldly church performs as the Lord wants it to: that is, to be light and salt, to wander doing good works as the Lord once did. I pray that the church will be able to present to everyone the gospel message of love and mercy and fulfill the effective and influential role the Lord destined for it. Thus, I invite each of us to get out of our solitary ship, out of our comfort zone, and begin to embark on a journey towards "the other" – a journey in which we vacate ourselves, instead elevating above our shoulders the message and mission of God towards his world and people.

Bibliography

'Abd El-'Aziz, Yasser. "Lemaza Yafoz Al-Isalmyyon?" [Why do Islamists win?]. *El-Maṣry El-Youm*, 15 January 2012. Accessed 25 November 2020. https://www.almasryalyoum.com/news/details/213767.

'Abd El-Fattaḥ, Nabil. "Oṭor Mo'assasyya: Al-Sa'i le Bena' Thaqafet Al-'ayesh Al-Moshtarak" [Foundational frameworks: Seeking to build the culture of coexistence]. Arab Center for Research and Studies. 12 June 2016. Accessed 24 April 2020. http://www.acrseg.org/40233.

'Abd el-Fattah, Samir. *Mabade' 'elm Al-ejetma'* [Principles of sociology]. Jordan: Dar Osama for Publishing & Distribution, 2006.

Ahmed, Khurshid. "Islam and the West: Confrontation or Cooperation?" *The Muslim World* 85, no. 1–2 (Jan–April 1995): 63–81.

'Alik, Aḥmed Muḥammad Yusef and al-Abshihi, Aḥmed Abd al-Hamid. *Al-Qyadah wa Tanmyat Al-Mojtama'* [Leadership and community development]. Cairo: Al-Mutanabi Library, 2013.

Al-Kāshf, Sayyida Ismā'il. *Misr al-Islāmiyya wa-a'hl al-Dhimma* [Islamic Egypt and al-Dhimmī people]. Cairo: The General Egyptian Institute for Books, 1993.

Al-Nujaihi, Mohamed. *Dor-Tarbya fel-tanmya Al-Ejtma'ya* [The role of pedagogy in the social development process]. Cairo: Dar Al-Nahḍah Al-Arabia, 1981.

———. *Dour Al-Ta'leem fi 'amalyet Al-Tanmya* [The role of education in the social development process]. Cairo: Dar Al-Nahḍah Al-Arabia, 1981.

Al-Samalouṭi, Nabil. *'elm Ejtma' Al-Tanmya* [Sociology of development]. Beirut: Dar Al-Nahḍah Al-'Arabia, 1981.

Ashgy, Bassam. "Al Ḥodor Al-Masiḥi fe Al-Sharq 'ansara Motajdeda: Resala Wa Shehada" [The Christian presence in the East: Renewed Pentecost, witness and message]. St. Terezia. Accessed 23 April 2020. http://www.terezia.com/section.php?id=523.

'Ashmāwī, Sa'īd. *Al-Islām al-Siyāsī* [Political Islam]. Cairo: Sina, 1989.

Barclay, William. *The Mind of Jesus*. London: SCM Press, 1960.

Bilbao, Jorge Rodriguez. "What Is the Territorial Approach to Local Development?" *Voices and Views* (blog). Capacity4dev, 18 February 2015.

Bradstock, Andrew and Hillary Russell. "Politics, Church, and the Common Good." In *A Companion to Public Theology*, edited by Sebastian Kim and Katie Day, 164–183. Boston, MA: Brill, 2017.

Campbell, Robert C. *Jesus Still Has Something to Say*. Valley Forge, PA: Judson Press, 1987.

Caragounis, C. C. "Kingdom of God/Heaven." In *Dictionary of Jesus and the Gospels*, edited by Joel B. Green and Scot McKnight, 420. Downers Grove, IL: InterVarsity Press, 1992.

Centers for Disease Control and Prevention. "Disability and Health Overview." Disability and Health Promotion. Last reviewed 16 September 2020. Accessed 25 November 2020. https://www.cdc.gov/ncbddd/disabilityandhealth/disability.html.

Chuma, Aeneas C. "Employment, Poverty Eradication and Inclusive Development." Special Session of the African Union Labour and Social Affairs Commission, Windhoek, Namibia, 23–25 April 2014. http://www.ilo.org/global/docs/WCMS_241717/lang--en/index.htm.

Deshbhratar, Anand Sukhadeo. "Missions and Religious Pluralism." Unpublished manuscript. Accessed 23 April 2020. https://www.academia.edu/16201355/MISSIONS_AND_RELIGIOUS_PLURALISM.

Diab, Muḥamed Ḥafez. *Sayyid Quṭb: Al-Khetab wa Al-Ideologia* [Sayyid Quṭb: Speech and ideology]. Beirut: Tale'a, 1988.

Dodd, Charles H. *The Parables of the Kingdom*. Welwyn: James Nisbet, 1950.

Dorgham, Raghda. "Makhawf Mn Taḥawl Al-Rabe' Al-'Arabi ela Rabe' Isalmi" [Fears of the Arab Spring turning into an Islamic Spring]. Wattan. 20 January 2012. https://www.wattan.net/ar/news/9631.html.

Duling, Dennis C. "The Kingdom of God in the Teaching of Jesus." *Word and World* 2, no. 2 (Spring 1982): 117–126.

Ela'lyan, A'bed Alla Ben A'lly. "Ṣdam El-Ḥadarat Wae'adat Sayaghet Al-Nezam El-Dwaly Al-Gadid" [The clash of civilizations and the remaking of the world order]. *Sector*, August 1988.

El-Daw, Fady. "Bayna Al-Lahot Al-Syasi wa Al-Syasa Al-lahotyya" [Between political theology and theological politics]. Ta'adodia (Plurism), 28 April 2017. Accessed 2 October 2019. https://taadudiya.com/بين-اللاهوت-السياسي-و-السياسة-اللاهوت/.

El Feqi, Moustafa. "Bal Hwa Rabe' 'Islami" [It is an Islamic Spring]. Maghress. Originally posted on Al-Ahdath, 15 March 2012. https://www.maghress.com/ahdathpress/38161.

Esposito, John L. *Islam: The Straight Path*. Oxford: Oxford University Press, 1991.

Gaiyed, Younis Laḥzy. "Nash't Al-Jam'yat Al-A'hlyya wa Taṭworha fi Miṣr" [The establishment and evolution of Christian civil associations in Egypt]. *The Journal of the Alexandria Church of the Coptic Catholics in Egypt* (1 January 2013). Accessed 11 November 2020. http://coptcatholic.net/p4256/.

Goldsworthy, G. "Kingdom of God." In *New Dictionary of Biblical Theology*, edited by T. Desmond Alexander and Brian S. Rosner, 619. Downers Grove, IL: InterVarsity Press, 2000.

Greene, Roberta R. "Resilience." In *The Encyclopedia of Social Work*, Vol. 3, edited by Terry Mizrahi and Donald M. Henderson, 526–531. Oxford: Oxford University Press, 2010.

Grigg, Viv. *Companion to the Poor*. Monrovia, CA: MARC, 1990.

Guthrie, Shirley. "Evangelism in a Pluralistic Society: A Reformed Perspective." Address to the 2002 Covenant Conference. Covenant Network of Presbyterians, 8 Nov. 2002. http://fpcshreveportblogs.org/wp-content/uploads/2010/11/Evangelism-

Pluralism.pdf. Accessed 11 January 2020. https://covnetpres.org/2002/11/08/evangelism-in-a-pluralistic-society/.

Ḥamoda, 'Adel. *Sayyid Quṭb: Min Al-Qaria Ela Al-Mashnaqa* [Sayyid Quṭb: From the village to the scaffold]. Cairo: Sina, 1987.

Harnack, Adolph. *What Is Christianity?* Trans. Thomas Bailey Saunders. London: G.P. Putnam & Sons, 1901.

Ḥassan, 'Abd el-Basset Moḥamed. *Al-Tanmya Al-Ejtma'yya* [Social development]. Cairo: Institute for Arab Research and Studies, 1993.

Hinson, Glenn. *The Integrity of the Church*. Nashville: Broadman Press, 1976.

Hujaila, Rahali and Boukhalfa Rafika. "Development Shifting from the Concept of Economy Development to the Concept of Human Development." *The Journal of Studies in Development and Society* (2016). Accessed 1 November 2019. https://www.univ-chlef.dz/eds/wp-content/uploads/2016/06/article N3.pdf.

Huntington, Samuel P. *The Clash of Civilizations and the Remaking of World Order*. New York: Simon and Schuster, 1996.

Husayn, Mir Zuhair. *Global Islamic Politics*. New York: Harper Collins, 1995.

Ibrahim, Sa'ad Eddin. *Egypt's Islamic Militant in Arab Society*. Edited by Nicholas S. Hopkins and Sa'ad Eddin Ibrahim. Cairo: The American University in Cairo Press, 1994.

Keck, Markus and Patrick Sakdapolrak. "What Is Social Resilience? Lessons Learned and Ways Forward." *Erdkunde* 67, no. 1 (2013): 5–19.

"A Kingdom Prayer." *Transformation* 11, no. 3 (July 1994): 2. https://doi.org/10.1177/026537889401100304.

Ladd, George Eldon. *Crucial Questions about the Kingdom of God*. Grand Rapids: Eerdmans, 1952.

———. *The Gospel of the Kingdom*. Grand Rapids: Eerdmans, 1959.

———. *The Presence of the Future*. Grand Rapids: Eerdmans, 1974.

Luomi, M., G. Fuller, L. Dahan, K. Lisboa Båsund, E. de la Mothe Karoubi, and G. Lafortune. *Arab Region SDG Index and Dashboards Report 2019*. Abu Dhabi and New York: Emirates Diplomatic Academy and Sustainable Development Solutions Network, 2019. https://s3.amazonaws.com/sustainabledevelopment.report/2019/2019_arab_region_index_and_dashboards.pdf.

Mathewes, Charles. *A Theology of Public Life*. Cambridge: Cambridge University Press, 2007.

McGrath, Alister E. "The Christian Church's Response to Pluralism." *Journal of the Evangelical Theology Society* 35, no. 4 (Dec. 1992): 487–501.

Mo'nes, Mona. "Miṣr fe 'ouon El-Gharab wa'ddaboh: sora maqbola le-Maser wa el-Islam" [Egypt in the eyes and the literature of the West: Acceptable images to Egypt and Islam]. *October*, May 1998.

Mussalli, Ahmed S. *Moderate and Radical Islamic Fundamentalism: The Quest for Modernity, Legitimacy, and the Islamic State*. Gainesville, FL: University Press of Florida, 1999.

Norris, Frederick W. "Mission and Religious Pluralism." *Leaven* 7, no. 1 (1999): 19–22. https://digitalcommons.pepperdine.edu/leaven/vol7/iss1/7.

Qolta, Youḥanna. *Naḥno wa Al-Akher* [We and the other]. Cairo: Dar El-Thaqafa Publishing, 2012.

Qonṣwa, Salaḥ. "Introduction." In *The Clash of Civilizations and the Remaking of World Order*, by Samuel P. Huntington. Arabic ed. Cairo: Al-Ahram, 1998.

Quṭb, Sayyid. *Al-Mostaqable le-haza al-Din* [The future for the religion]. Cairo: Dar El-Shorouk, 1988.

———. *Ma 'ālim fī El-Tarīq* [Milestones]. Cairo: Dar El-Shorouk, 1972.

———. *Ma'rikat al-Islam wa al-Ra'smalya* [The battle of Islam and capitalism]. Cairo: Dar El-Shorouk, 1987.

———. *Naḥwa Mojatam'a Islamy* [Towards the Islamic society]. Cairo: Dar El-Shorouk, 1988.

Rauschenbusch, Walter. *Christianity: The Social Order*. London: Macmillan, 1912.

"Religious Plurality and Christian Self-Understanding." World Council of Churches. 14 February 2006. https://www.oikoumene.org/resources/documents/religious-plurality-and-christian-self-understanding.

Ritschl, Albert. *The Christian Doctrine of Justification and Reconciliation*. Edinburgh: Scribner's, 1900.

Rivera, Joseph. *Political Theology and Pluralism: Renewing Public Dialogue*. Dublin: Palgrave Macmillan, 2018.

Roy, Olivier. *The Failure of Political Islam*. London: I.B. Tauris Publishers, 1994.

Shafik, Mohamed. *Social Development: Studies in Development Issues and Community Problems*. Cairo: Modern University Office, 1994.

Shoe'ir, Ṣalaḥ. "Al Jam'eyat Al-Ahlyh bi Miṣr Tqom Bedawr Tkafoly, wa Toḥareb alfqr, wa Tahtam bel-Mra'h" [NGOs in Egypt play a symbiotic role, fight poverty, and take care of women]. *The Civilized Dialogue*, no. 5360 (December 2016). Accessed 25 November 2020. http://www.ahewar.org/debat/show.art.asp?aid=540096. http://www.ahewar.org/debat/show.art.asp?aid=540096.

Sider, Ronald. *One-Sided Christianity?: Uniting the Church to Heal a Lost and Broken World*. Grand Rapids: Zondervan, 1993.

Sivan, Emmanuel. *Radical Islam Medieval Theology and Modern Politics*. New Haven: Yale University Press, 1985.

Suchocki, Marjorie Hewitt. *Divinity and Diversity: A Christian Affirmation of Religious Pluralism*. Nashville: Abingdon Press, 2003.

Thielman, Frank. *Theology of the New Testament: A Canonical and Synthetic Approach*. Grand Rapids: Zondervan, 2005.

The Third Lausanne Congress. *The Cape Town Commitment*. Bodmin: Printbridge, 2011.

United Nations. "Community Development." UNTERM: The United Nations Terminology Database. Archived from the original 14 July 2014. Accessed 29 April 2020. https://web.archive.org/web/20140714225617/http://unterm.un.org/

DGAACS/unterm.nsf/8fa942046ff7601c85256983007ca4d8/526c2eaba978f0078 52569fd00036819?OpenDocument.

———. "Green Economy." Sustainable Development Goals Knowledge Platform. Accessed 25 November 2020. https://sustainabledevelopment.un.org/topics/greeneconomy.

———. "United Nations Conference on Sustainable Development, Rio+20." Sustainable Development Goals Knowledge Platform. https://sustainabledevelopment.un.org/rio20.

United Nations Development Programme. *Arab Human Development Report 2002: Creating Opportunities for Future Generations*. New York: UNDP and RBAS, 2002.

Van Groen, Dick and Patrick Cramp. "The Impact Study of Community Development Approaches Applied to Development in the Coptic Evangelical Commission." Report presented to EZE, CEOSS, and Bread for the World. Egypt, 1998.

Virtue, David W. *A Vision of Hope*. Oxford: Regnum Books, 1996.

Weiss, Johannes. *Jesus' Proclamation of the Kingdom of God*. Grand Rapids: Eerdmans, 1971.

Willis, Wendell, ed. *The Kingdom of God in 20th-Century Interpretation*. Peabody, MA: Hendrickson, 1987.

World Health Organization. "Blindness and Vision Impairment," 8 October 2020. Accessed 25 November 2020. https://www.who.int/news-room/fact-sheets/detail/blindness-and-visual-impairment.

Wright, Christopher. *Integral Mission and the Great Commission: Integrating our Mission with God's Mission*. Lausanne: Lausanne-Orthodox Initiative, 2014.

Zakaria, Fou'ad. "Ḥadaratna wa Mafhom el-Seraʻ" [Our culture and the concept of conflict]. *El-Moswer*, July 1998.

———. "Thaqaft El-Mokabarat el-Markazia wa mafhom seraʻel ḥadarat" [The culture of central intelligence and the concept of the clash of civilizations]. *El-Moswer*, June 1998.

Zaki, Andrea. *Al-Aqbaṭ wa Al-Thawra* [The Copts and the revolution]. Cairo: Dar El-Thaqafa Publishing, 2015.

———. "Al Masyḥyoun Al-ʻarab wal Mowaṭana" [Arab Christians and citizenship]. In *Al-Tafsseer Al-ʻarabi Al-Moʻaser lelketab Al-Moqaddas* [The Arabic contemporary commentary on the Bible], edited by Andrea Zaki, 2077. Cairo: Dar El-Thaqafa Publishing House, 2018.

———. "Al ʻaysh Al Moshtarak" [Coexistence]. In *Al-Tafsseer Al-ʻarabi Al-Moʻaser lelketab Al-Moqaddas* [The Arabic contemporary commentary on the Bible], edited by Andrea Zaki, 57. Cairo: Dar El-Thaqafa Publishing House, 2018.

———. "Middle Eastern and Arab Theology." In *Global Dictionary of Theology*, edited by William A. Dyrness and Veli-Matti Karkkainen, 537–538. Chicago, IL: InterVarsity Press, 1992.

Langham Literature and its imprints are a ministry of Langham Partnership.

Langham Partnership is a global fellowship working in pursuit of the vision God entrusted to its founder John Stott –

to facilitate the growth of the church in maturity and Christ-likeness through raising the standards of biblical preaching and teaching.

Our vision is to see churches in the Majority World equipped for mission and growing to maturity in Christ through the ministry of pastors and leaders who believe, teach and live by the word of God.

Our mission is to strengthen the ministry of the word of God through:
- nurturing national movements for biblical preaching
- fostering the creation and distribution of evangelical literature
- enhancing evangelical theological education

especially in countries where churches are under-resourced.

Our ministry

Langham Preaching partners with national leaders to nurture indigenous biblical preaching movements for pastors and lay preachers all around the world. With the support of a team of trainers from many countries, a multi-level programme of seminars provides practical training, and is followed by a programme for training local facilitators. Local preachers' groups and national and regional networks ensure continuity and ongoing development, seeking to build vigorous movements committed to Bible exposition.

Langham Literature provides Majority World preachers, scholars and seminary libraries with evangelical books and electronic resources through publishing and distribution, grants and discounts. The programme also fosters the creation of indigenous evangelical books in many languages, through writer's grants, strengthening local evangelical publishing houses, and investment in major regional literature projects, such as one volume Bible commentaries like *The Africa Bible Commentary* and *The South Asia Bible Commentary*.

Langham Scholars provides financial support for evangelical doctoral students from the Majority World so that, when they return home, they may train pastors and other Christian leaders with sound, biblical and theological teaching. This programme equips those who equip others. Langham Scholars also works in partnership with Majority World seminaries in strengthening evangelical theological education. A growing number of Langham Scholars study in high quality doctoral programmes in the Majority World itself. As well as teaching the next generation of pastors, graduated Langham Scholars exercise significant influence through their writing and leadership.

To learn more about Langham Partnership and the work we do visit **langham.org**

www.ingramcontent.com/pod-product-compliance
Lightning Source LLC
Chambersburg PA
CBHW071450150426
43191CB00008B/1297